PRAISE FOR *THE RISING WATER TRILOGY*

RISING WATER

"[*Rising Water*] grabbed the audience in its first tense moments and never let go. Biguenet has created characters of such opposite dimensions that they generate innate humor, which continues deeper into the play than one would have thought possible. It is natural and needed; otherwise the situation would be unbearable."—*New Orleans Times-Picayune*

"[*Rising Water*] is . . . indelible an experience."—*Backstage.com* (Los Angeles)

"John Biguenet's play about a middle-aged couple trapped in an attic after Hurricane Katrina has the makings of an American theatrical classic."—*Baton Rouge Advocate*

"*Rising Water* emerges as a great American play—perhaps one of the first great plays of the twenty-first century."—*Orange County Register*

SHOTGUN

"In *Shotgun* . . . playwright John Biguenet exposes with power and grace the wounds that remain and examines how they might best be healed."—*New Orleans Times-Picayune*

"*Shotgun* . . . deals with race but is ultimately about people. And it's fascinating."—*Gambit Weekly*

"[*Shotgun* is] a serious play about serious subjects, and yet it is filled with the rich dark humor that got New Orleanians through those days after the storm."—*Nola.com*

"Biguenet's ear for dramatic, natural dialogue is so adroit you cannot turn your eyes and mind from his play."—*WYES-TV*

"It's the narrow focus of this new play that shakes you. . . . Human drama doesn't have to look huge to be heartbreaking."—*Orlando Sentinel*

"A moving exploration of a ravaged New Orleans . . . [and] an absorbing new drama by John Biguenet."—*Sarasota Herald-Tribune*

MOLD

"Summoning up deeply set, perhaps nearly forgotten, feelings of anger, regret and sorrow, but also hope and humor, with *Mold*, Biguenet has completed his trilogy on Katrina and its aftermath. It may well be regarded as the finest artistic achievement expressing the personal impact the flood had—and continues to have—on our lives today."—*New Orleans Times-Picayune*

"Intimate and intense . . . [*Mold*] resounds with authenticity and insight."—*NOLA Defender*

"Original theater at its best . . . [is] Biguenet's fascinating play. Go see it."—*Gambit Weekly*

"A wonderful play."—*WYES-TV*

THE RISING WATER TRILOGY

THE RISING WATER TRILOGY

——— P L A Y S ———

JOHN BIGUENET

With a Foreword by George Judy

LOUISIANA STATE UNIVERSITY PRESS   BATON ROUGE

Published with the assistance of the Borne Fund

Published by Louisiana State University Press
Copyright © 2015, 2014, 2013, 2009, 2007 by John Biguenet

Designer: Barbara Neely Bourgoyne
Typeface: Ingeborg

Library of Congress Cataloging-in-Publication Data
Biguenet, John.
 [Plays. Selections]
 The Rising Water trilogy : plays / John Biguenet ; with a foreword by George Judy.
   pages cm
 Includes bibliographical references and index.
 ISBN 978-0-8071-6195-1 (cloth : alk. paper) — ISBN 978-0-8071-6140-1 (pbk. : alk. paper) — ISBN 978-0-8071-6141-8 (pdf) — ISBN 978-0-8071-6142-5 (epub) — ISBN 978-0-8071-6143-2 (mobi)
 I. Title.
 PS3552.I424A6 2015
 812'.54—dc23

2014048993

"This is the first time that the Corps has had to stand up and say, 'We've had a catastrophic failure.'"

—LT. GEN. CARL A. STROCK, COMMANDING GENERAL
U.S. Army Corps of Engineers
June 1, 2006

---

*These plays are dedicated to
the victims of this manmade disaster.*

CONTENTS

FOREWORD

The legacy of Hurricane Katrina, like the roots of the mold described in the third play of John Biguenet's *Rising Water Trilogy*, has entrenched itself in both the reality and mythology of New Orleans, of Louisiana, and of the world. Almost no major disaster—natural or manmade—in the near decade since the fall of the levees in that terrible August of 2005 has escaped comparison with the nightmare that consumed and still consumes one of our great cities. The suffering, the anger, the frustration—as well as the hope and humor—of citizens trapped in that nightmare have resonated worldwide and served as a call to arms against the ineptitude and injustice of our political and social bureaucracies, even as it also calls attention to the many heroic individuals who serve within those institutions. Despite the wealth of images and descriptions that followed in the wake of Katrina, *The Rising Water Trilogy* has captured a truth that is at once both more "real" and more "poetic"—and thus perhaps more transcendently truthful than any other account in my experience. These plays, particularly as shared in production, are undeniably human, deceptively complex, and informed by the specific and deeply personal experience of the playwright. Like the disaster, they offer no easy answers, but challenge us to ask better questions about our lives, our communities, and our responsibilities to each other. The plays are a fine artistic accomplishment, but equally they are a powerful historical document of a troubled time, with significant implications for political and social change.

Rising Water, the first of the three plays, as one reviewer has already suggested, "emerges as a great American play—perhaps one of the first great plays of the twenty-first century" (*Orange County Register*). This assessment will be shared by many, and this work holds its own in comparison to many of the great plays of the last century, combining as it does the social specificity and personality of *The Price,* by Arthur Miller, with the lyric language of Tennessee Williams, who also knew and loved New Orleans, and the humor and existential searching of Samuel Beckett. High praise indeed! Having both directed and performed this piece no doubt colors my flush of enthusiasm, but my experience of living the lives of these characters in the theater was one of confronting profound questions while experiencing the detail of truthful moment-to-moment life that only comes from characters created from a genuine sense of lives grounded in specific place, time, and circumstances. These people are REAL, and my own experience was borne out each evening in the theater as members of the audience experienced Sugar and Camille, the couple trapped by the relentlessly rising water, as if they were their own neighbors, family, or friends fighting for their lives and redressing old and lingering wounds. Inevitably, after each performance, people waited to share their own version of what they experienced in braving the storm and its aftermath, and we were struck each time by how their stories echoed the play: the family relationships, the terror, and the love that sustained them through the night. It was a joy to see them respond to their stories, stories that were true to them but that they had not been able to put into words, rendered in compelling and truthful life in *Rising Water*. The universality of that experience makes the play enthralling for audiences worldwide, but for those who lived through the reality of Katrina, it captures a definitive social history.

Shotgun, the second play of the trio, follows the chronology of the Katrina experience four months after the levee collapse, and captures the same sense of specific reality as the first play—the despair and confusion of a city still reeling and survivors groping for a place to put their feet, not to mention their lives. Moving from the attic and roof of the home depicted in *Rising Water* into the "shotgun" duplex referred to in the title, the play reflects both a city and a house divided. More traditional in structure than the first play, it is no less moving in its depiction of family and of the divisions both created and revealed by the pressures of Katrina's waters. Parent and child relationships, the loss of mothers and wives, suggested in *Rising Water*, here take a primary focus, balanced with the central relationship that grows between landlady Mattie and tenant Beau, as scenes shift back and forth between the two sides of the shotgun and reveal characters that refuse to be pigeonholed as hero or villain. Biguenet does a splendid balancing act in keeping the characters complicated while giving us a sense of satisfaction in their struggle to meet their immediate needs, exacerbated by the legacy of the flood. Politics and bureaucracy come in for more direct incrimination in this second play of the trilogy, as time now has allowed the "truth" about the causes of the flood, the magnitude of the losses, and the ineptitude of response to the survivors to come into view. The play absolutely captures the intergenerational anger, the inflamed prejudice, and the weariness and despair for the future that pervaded New Orleans soon after the disaster. It equally reveals the courage, humor, generosity and self-awareness that let many keep putting one foot in front of the other on a march back to sanity and stability—for some literally the only path available. Extremely effective in the theater, *Shotgun* creates a telling social snapshot of New Orleans those months after the storm, and makes clear that the receding waters of Katrina marked only the beginning of the real disaster.

Finally, *Mold* completes the trilogy with a powerful depiction of New Orleans nearly a year after the waters had submerged much of the city. The central characters, Trey and Marie, unlike the characters in the previous two plays, left the day before the storm and have lived in Houston for the past months, returning only for the funeral of Trey's parents, lost in the rising waters of Katrina. In the iconic image of the abandoned and broken family home covered in mold to which the couple return, New Orleans is revealed, as the playwright describes, as a city "where the violent death rate surpasses Baghdad's at the height of the suicide bombings that summer, where the economy is in ruins, and the ground—saturated with heavy metals and other toxins from the flood—is unfit for children." This is the angriest of the plays in the trilogy and rightly so, as the full extent of damage, personal loss, and the incapacity of our institutions to solve the real problems of victims had at this point become increasingly tragic and real. At the same time the endless avoidance, behind technicality and bureaucracy, of responsibility in meeting the needs of the community had become increasingly absurd. Rather than simply railing against societal inadequacy in response to disaster (which it skewers with great humor), the play calls all of us to examine our own guilt, our own difficult choices, our need to protect our children and to define what truly makes a place our home. *Mold* captures this time in New Orleans in its character portraits, again revealing human beings of dimension rather than types, but the play transcends the specific social moment in its depiction of our emotional connection to literal places that hold value unseen and inexplicable to the "outsider." Like the mold itself, this value is rooted in our bones, in our DNA—for better or for worse—or perhaps for better AND for worse.

The plays of John Biguenet's trilogy, in addition to being fine theater, form a fascinating, detailed, and human revelation of a particular year in Louisiana history, but also transcend that place and era to speak to global as well as intensely personal issues surrounding both natural and manmade disasters. These plays bear reading as history, sociology, and anthropology as well as drama, but their triumph is to inform our discussion of how to respond in the wake of disaster and deeply humanize what might have become simply a statistical portrait of destruction along the Gulf Coast. That loss of humanity would be as great a tragedy as the rising waters of Katrina.

GEORGE JUDY

ACKNOWLEDGMENTS

Theater is a collaborative art form, and so I have many individuals to thank. The continuing support of my agents, Ron Gwiazda and Amy Wagner, at Abrams Artists began when Ron came to New Orleans and saw the original production of *Rising Water* at Southern Rep Theatre. Southern Rep itself, under the artistic direction of first Ryan Rilette and then Aimée Hayes, has premiered all three plays under the difficult circumstances the city has faced since the levee collapse in 2005. Southern Rep is a member of the National New Play Network, "an alliance of theaters dedicated to the development, production, and continued life of new plays." NNPN awarded *Rising Water* its Annual Commission in 2006 and selected the play for presentation at the 2006 National Showcase of New Plays. NNPN awarded *Shotgun* its Continued Life of New Plays Fund Award to help support its first three productions at Southern Rep Theatre, the Orlando Shakespeare Theater, and Florida Studio Theatre. Other NNPN theaters have either mounted productions or presented staged readings of the plays in the trilogy, including (in addition to those already cited) New Jersey Repertory Company, Playwrights Theatre of New Jersey, and Unicorn Theatre. Many other theaters have mounted productions of the plays, as well, such as Storefront Theatre, Acting Unlimited, Swine Palace Theatre, Edward Lewis Black Theater Festival, Theatre Las Vegas, Different Strokes Performing Arts Collective, the University of North Carolina—Charlotte, Congo Square Theatre, Bayou Playhouse, Shadowland Theatre, Louisiana State University—Baton Rouge, Maverick Theater, and Vineyard Playhouse. I am grateful not only to the artistic directors of all these theaters but also to the directors, actors, designers, and staff members who brought these three plays to the stage. Finally, MaryKatherine Callaway, Director of the LSU Press, has been an enthusiastic supporter of the publication of the trilogy; I very much appreciate the efforts of MaryKatherine and her staff to produce this book.

THE RISING WATER TRILOGY

INTRODUCTION

FROM RAGE TO PAGE TO STAGE TO RAGE

When I began what would become a trilogy of plays about the flooding of New Orleans and its aftermath, we had been displaced since the levee collapse months before, our house still rank with mold even though my wife, our son, and I had gutted much of it. Sleeping at first in a day-care center that lacked hot water and finally finding a vacant three-room shotgun to rent, we salvaged what we could of our lives.

Earlier, while still exiled from my hometown by martial law, I had been asked by the *New York Times* to serve as its first guest columnist. Writing for the *Times* that sweltering October in the daycare center—sitting on a twelve-inch-high blue plastic chair with my portable computer on a barely taller red plastic table—I documented life in a ruined city as dazed survivors wandered home from shelters across the country. The more I reported on what had happened, however, the more I began to doubt the official explanations of how a great American city had been destroyed and nearly fifteen hundred American citizens had drowned or died of dehydration in attics and on rooftops as they awaited help that never came.

As the first anniversary of the disaster approached, I wrote a column that began, "Most of what you think you know about what happened in New Orleans a year ago is probably wrong." For most Americans, that continues to be true.

The city did receive a glancing blow from the weak side of Hurricane Katrina as the storm moved up the Mississippi-Louisiana state line. However, as *USA Today* reported, the highest sustained winds measured in New Orleans were only 95 miles per hour, making Katrina a strong Category 1 hurricane and thus likely to cause "minimal" to "moderate" damage. And that's exactly what the storm did.

But in the hours after the hurricane had moved north of the city, the failure of defective levees designed and built by the U.S. Army Corps of Engineers inundated 80 percent of New Orleans, an area seven times the size of Manhattan, with saltwater up to fourteen feet deep. Having resisted the accumulating evidence for nine months, insisting over and over again that the levees had been overtopped rather than breached at the base, the narrative of Corps spokespersons and their allies in Congress drowned out the more complicated truth. When Lt. Gen. Carl Strock, its commandant, finally admitted in June 2006 that the U.S. Army Corps of Engineers was responsible for most of the flooding of New Orleans and the attendant deaths and destruction, the nation had already moved on to other issues.

By the time I wrote that anniversary column in August of 2006, I had begun *Rising Water*, a play about a couple trapped in their attic and then on their rooftop by the flood. An earlier column I had written back in mid-October 2005 entitled "How They Died" explained that it was well into the night after the hurricane before the floodwater reached some neighborhoods, but then rose as quickly as eight feet in ten minutes. My column concluded, "So I imagine that's how they died, many of the drowned, trapped in a dark house or in a pitch-black attic, if they made it that far, as water rushed in from failed levees our government could not find the funds to strengthen."

In the spring of 2005, Ryan Rilette, then the artistic director of Southern Rep Theatre, had produced my play *The Vulgar Soul*, based on *Wundmale*, a radio drama I had written for Westdeutscher Rundfunk, the German radio network. The tale of a stigmatic with no religious faith, *The Vulgar Soul* became the bestselling new play in Southern Rep's twenty-year history. When I mentioned my idea for *Rising Water* to him after he and his family had returned to New Orleans, he said to put aside everything else I was writing and Southern Rep would produce the play.

My first drafts were so angry that I kept killing off the couple in the first act, prompting Ryan to ask what he was supposed to do for a second act. Little by little, though, the characters took on greater dimension, and I wrote myself and my anger off the stage.

One of these later drafts won the 2006 Annual Commission award of the National New Play Network and an invitation to present a staged reading of *Rising Water* at NNPN's National Showcase of New Plays at New Jersey Rep that winter. The consensus of the talkback following the performance was to make my script more universal by pushing further in the direction of absurdism—even though I was talking about actual events.

On the plane back to New Orleans from Newark, however, I decided to do just the opposite. Instead of making it more universal, I would make it more local. I would write a play for New Orleanians about New Orleanians performed by New Orleanians. It would be a gift to the city. I expected a small, single run.

Because I could find nothing in the canon of American literature or theater that offered a model for the structuring of a play about the destruction of an entire city, I turned to world literature. I found in postwar Germany and Japan after the Kobe earthquake a striking similarity in the response of their writers. Narratives about the catastrophes in those countries invariably drew upon elements of their mythologies. For example, Günter Grass's *The Tin Drum* is narrated by the diminutive Oskar, a character surely drawn from the dwarfs of the *Nibelungenlied* and other early Germanic literature. And a story in Haruki Murakami's *After the Quake* relates how Tokyo is saved from annihilation when a giant worm intent on the city's destruction is defeated, though—as in so many samurai tales—at the cost of the hero's life.

Approaching only the three hundredth anniversary of its founding, New Orleans lacks an ancient mythology. But the iconic images of New Orleanians stranded on their rooftops by the flood suggested that our architecture, expressive of both our climate and our culture, might serve as a formative principle for my story.

As I considered a first act set in a dark attic into which the couple has fled and a second act on a starlit rooftop as the water continues to rise, I realized that the attic, a repository of the souvenirs of their life together, is an embodiment of memory; the roof, opening on an unimaginable scene of devastation, is the setting of a dream. Hunched over in the dark past of their lives, Sugar and his wife, Camille, recall their thirty years together. Although Camille is slender enough to slip onto the roof through the hole Sugar has crafted, he is too heavy for any more than his head to fit through the jagged opening. Standing beneath a sky full of stars, his wife wonders whether he might have been right when he had earlier suggested in the attic that "Maybe it's not the end of the world that's going on outside. Maybe it could be for us a new world just beginning." But trapped between the past and a future he cannot reach, Sugar begins to understand that for him, at least, it may well be the end of the world.

Southern Rep Theatre was located, at that time, in Canal Place, an upscale mall on the edge of the French Quarter. Having been looted in the chaos that descended upon the city as it flooded, the mall was then set afire by fleeing looters. When the play opened just eighteen months later, we could still smell the smoke as we awaited our first audience.

With the city reduced to less than half of its preflood population, much of Southern Rep's subscription base was gone. But Ryan was committed to the theater's mission of serving the community, especially in the midst of a continuing crisis, and assembled the resources to mount a production.

We were, of course, very conscious of the effect the play might have on an audience that had so recently lived through the event it depicted. We even discussed inviting grief counselors to moderate the matinee talkbacks we had scheduled. But still, we were unprepared when a news crew from a local television station had to interrupt filming a brief clip from the play during rehearsal because the cameraman had begun to sob so hard he couldn't hold his camera steady.

From its opening night until the show closed two months later, we had a full house at every performance. And what happened at the end of the first preview happened after every performance. *Rising Water* closes with Sugar and Camille, stranded on their rooftop and aware that no help is on its way, singing a song they had argued about earlier, "If Ever I Cease to Love." But their singing is drowned out by the wail of house alarms going off all across the city as the backup batteries die. With the shriek of those piercing sirens rising, the couple turn away from each other and face the audience. In the sudden blackout that followed, there was never any applause. Only as the lights rose for the actors' curtain call would someone in the audience stand and begin to clap until the entire audience were on their feet.

But then, instead of leaving, nearly all of the audience would sink back into their chairs again. The night of that first preview, though no talkback had been planned, Ryan hesitantly stepped onto the stage and asked if anyone would like to talk about what had just been seen. Some commented on the play, but most talked about what had happened to them, to their families, to their neighbors. Nearly an hour later, Ryan brought the discussion to a close. A few people were still crying.

It went on like that for the entire run—talkbacks and tears at nearly every performance. When Southern Rep finally closed the show because of a contractual commitment for another production, I thought that would be the end of *Rising Water*. I had begun another play, *Night Train*, set in a European train compartment; I thought I was finished with the flooding of New Orleans.

At the end of the summer, the National Theatre invited me to London on a Studio Attachment to develop *Night Train*. While at the National, I showed my director, Charlotte Gwinner, the opening pages of a play I had begun entitled *Shotgun*, set in New Orleans a few months after the levee collapse. Charlotte was extremely enthusiastic about the script and urged me to finish it when I returned to the States.

In the meantime, I had begun to receive inquiries from theaters about *Rising Water*. I doubted whether the play would work for audiences outside New Orleans, but there have now been eighteen full productions and staged readings around the U.S. In the talkbacks I have attended, audiences invariably begin by expressing their surprise. "I had no idea that's what happened in New Orleans," one audience member at Kansas City's Unicorn Theatre said. "I thought a hurricane flooded the city."

By the summer of 2008 in New Orleans, a bitter exhaustion had set in. A study that year publicized by the National Institute of Mental Health found that contrary to previous disaster experience in which "the prevalence of mental disorders among the survivors gradually decreases and fades out after about two years," the rate of serious mental illness in the area had increased compared to one year after the levee collapse, with the prevalence of suicidal thoughts more than doubling and actual suicidal planning nearly tripling. As New Orleanians joked, "There's nothing post about our PTSD."

An earlier study published in 2007 in the *Journal of Urban Health* examining post-traumatic stress disorder in the New Orleans workforce found a strong relationship between PTSD symptoms and living in temporary housing.

Of course, none of us living among the ruins of New Orleans needed scientific studies to tell us what we were feeling. It was clear that, at least emotionally, life in the city was growing more difficult. The story of the flood was not approaching a conclusion; in fact, we began to understand that we were still at the beginning.

For the first few months after the levee collapse, old animosities were eclipsed by the desperation of daily life. But once the mayor, facing a difficult reelection bid, made his "Chocolate City" speech in mid-January 2006, warning black New Orleanians that Uptown whites were seeking to keep them from returning to their homes, racial distrust overwhelmed the city.

Shotgun knits together the story of exhausted survivors four months after the flood seeking a place to sleep as they begin to tally their losses. Continuing the architectural motif I had employed in *Rising Water* as a structural device, I used the most typical of New Orleans houses, the "double shotgun," as it's called in the city, as a model for the play's narrative form. The shotgun, a narrow house in which room follows room without an interior hallway, was designed in response to the limited land available for development in a city surrounded by water. The double shotgun is a duplex in which a second side mirrors the first, with one side rented and the other often occupied by the property's owner.

The play alternates scenes between the shared porch of the house and the kitchen of the rental side. A white man and his teenage son, having lost their house in the flood, rent half of the shotgun double from a young African American woman, whose father has lost his house in the Lower Ninth Ward and moved in with his daughter. Eventually, the white man and his black landlady fall in love, but no one is happy for them. When he tries to persuade her father that the world has changed—"Look at us, you and me, black and white, living here together under one roof"—the old man retorts, "Yeah, with a wall running between us."

The effect of the play on its audience was similar to that of *Rising Water*—and not just in New Orleans. Winning a Continued Life of New Plays Fund award from the National New Play Network, *Shotgun* had a "rolling world premiere," as NNPN calls it, at Southern Rep, Orlando Shakespeare Theater, and Florida Studio Theatre. The first act concludes with a searing monologue about the death of the man's wife in the aftermath of the levee collapse, a death for which his son holds him responsible. At a performance I attended in Orlando, a woman next to me in the audience began to weep as the lights faded. The same thing happened in Sarasota and New Orleans. Like *Rising Water*, it continues to be performed, having now had a dozen productions and staged readings around the country.

In *Mold*, the final play of the trilogy, I again turned to architecture to find a central image of the conflict faced by the characters; in this case, it is a family home in ruins and encrusted in mold. Returning for the first time nearly a year after the levee collapse, a young husband is forced to choose between his wife and the city he loves. Facing an incompetent government bureaucracy and a bottom-line insurance company, the man, whose parents died of dehydration in their attic during the flood, cannot bring himself to abandon the house and the city in which he grew up. His wife, though, can no longer justify life in a city where the violent death rate surpasses Baghdad's at the height of the suicide bombings that summer, where the economy is in ruins, and where the earth itself—saturated with heavy metals and other toxins from the flood—is unfit for children.

Mold premiered at Southern Rep in 2013. Although eight years had passed since defective levees collapsed and destroyed most of the city, the wounds still opened easily here in New Orleans. The actors quickly learned to ignore sobbing in the darkened theater, and we began to expect that some members of the audience would choose to sit out the second act in the lobby, waiting as friends and family returned to the auditorium to watch the conclusion of the play.

One year after the levee collapse, I concluded my series of columns for the *New York Times* with a final piece entitled "What Have I Learned?" If I ask myself that same question about the three plays I have written, I must begin by admitting that writing has not healed whatever wounds I carry; in fact, writing these plays has felt more like salt than balm. The deeper I have explored the needless suffering of my fellow New Orleanians, the angrier I have grown.

But I have learned that when a culture is in crisis, when a city has been destroyed, artists are as necessary to its rebuilding as carpenters and plumbers and roofers. The playwrights and musicians and photographers and poets and painters and novelists and filmmakers of New Orleans put aside their personal projects to depict what their fellow citizens were enduring and to pose the questions the community needed to address. The response of their audiences was telling. Before the flood, such artists might have received expressions of admiration for their work. But now, even ten years later, people on the street express not their admiration but their gratitude.

As my wife and I have watched couple after couple break up under the stress of lost homes and lost jobs and lost self-esteem, I've discovered that if one wants to depict the human toll of a massive disaster, its effect on relationships is the most visible embodiment of that catastrophe. I could not have guessed before the flood that in composing a trilogy about the destruction of a city, I would wind up writing three love stories.

I've also learned that plays are connected to the life of a particular city in ways that other forms of narrative are not. When productions of the plays in this trilogy were mounted in New Jersey, Florida, Missouri, California, I urged the directors not to let the actors fabricate an exotic New Orleans accent but to allow audiences to hear something of their own English in the dialogue on stage.

Because in the end, what happened in New Orleans is not about New Orleans. When a country fails to maintain its infrastructure, when it ignores climate change, when it deprofessionalizes government service because of ideological contempt for governance itself, when it allows poverty to fester, when it encourages racism through coded speech, when it refuses to hold responsible for the consequences of their policies those leaders who devised them, then what happened in August 2005 is not about the place where it happened. It's about the people who let it happen. And because no one was held accountable, it will happen again.

New Orleans is simply where the future arrived first.

RISING WATER

Rising Water was originally commissioned by Southern Rep Theatre, Ryan Rilette, Producing Artistic Director, and Aimée Hayes, Managing Director. This commission was funded in part by a grant from the National New Play Network. The world premiere of *Rising Water* was produced by Southern Rep Theatre in New Orleans on March 14, 2007. It was directed by Ryan Rilette with the following cast:

CAMILLE..............................Cristine McMurdo-Wallis
SUGAR..Danny Bowen

Scenic design by Geoffrey Hall
Lighting design by William Liotta
Costumes by Michelle Bohn
Sound design by Jack Daniel Stanley
Production Stage Manager: Michelle Kelleher

CAMILLE, slender but no longer young

SUGAR, her husband, no longer young or slender

PLACE

New Orleans.

TIME

August 2005.

ACT I

SCENE 1

(The dark attic of a narrow, one-story house at night about 2:00 a.m., cluttered with old possessions. Moonlight sifts in through a vent in the roof. The sound of a folding staircase being pulled down suddenly and splashing into water. CAMILLE clambers up from below into the attic, a flashlight on in her hand. The bottom of her nightgown is wet.)

CAMILLE *(shouting down the folding stairs)*: The flashlight, Sugar. Bring the light. It's dark up here.

SUGAR *(from below)*: I thought you brought it up with you.

CAMILLE: Not this light. The other one.

SUGAR *(from below)*: Which one?

CAMILLE: The one that's in the kitchen. Hurry, though. The water's everywhere.

SUGAR *(from below, sloshing through water)*: I know, I know. But I can't see a goddamn thing down here. Where'd you say you put it?

CAMILLE *(pointing her flashlight down the stairs)*: I didn't put it anywhere. Why would I move it? The flashlight's in the cupboard above the oven where it always is.

(Long, anxious pause.)

Sug?

(Silence.)

Is it where I said it was?

(*Silence.*)

Sugar, did you find it there?

(*Silence.*)

Sug?

SUGAR (*from below*): I got it, yeah, I found it where you said.

CAMILLE: You scared me half to death. Now come up here. The water's rising all around the stairs.

SUGAR (*from below*): Wait. Let me grab the photographs.

CAMILLE: Photographs? Just get up here.

SUGAR (*from below*): The albums in the bookcase, I'm talking about.

CAMILLE: We had them on the bottom shelf. They're ruined by now. Just get yourself up here before you drown.

SUGAR (*from below*): Then what about that box of pictures in Frankie's room?

CAMILLE (*pointing her flashlight down the stairs again*): There isn't time. (*Pause.*) Sugar, I can see the water coming up.

(*Silence.*)

Sug?

(*Silence.*)

You hear me, Sug? Forget the photographs.

(*Silence.*)

Sugar, you scaring me.

(*Long silence.*)

SUGAR (*from below*): They weren't there. You remember where you seen them last?

CAMILLE: I don't know. Just climb up here. The water's getting higher all the time.

SUGAR (*from below*): There's one more place they might be—on top the cabinet in the dining room.

CAMILLE: Sug, leave them be.

SUGAR (*from below*): Just let me look. I think I saw them there last week.

CAMILLE: The water's coming up the stairs. Will you forget those photographs? They're not worth drowning for.

(*Silence.*)

Sugar?

(*Long silence.*)

Sug?

(*Silence.*)

Sugar!

SUGAR (*from below, but more distant*): Will you calm down, Camille?

(*Pause, then approaching the bottom of the stairs.*)

I found them where I thought they were. Just hold your horses. I'm coming up.

(*His legs wet, SUGAR climbs up into the attic with his flashlight on, clasping a box of photos to his chest.*)

There. You happy now?

CAMILLE: You make me crazy. Why you have to be so damn hard-headed all the time? Water's pouring in downstairs from God knows where, and you decide to go wandering around in the dark. You lucky you didn't drown or something.

SUGAR: A little water's all it is down there.

CAMILLE: A little? Think you're fooling me with that?

SUGAR: Now don't go getting all hysterical on me, Camille. We got a little water in the house is all. No point making more of it than what it is.

CAMILLE: Listen, Sug, when you woke me up with all that snoring of yours and I swung my legs out of bed, I stepped in water halfway up my knees. Scared the daylights out of me, but it couldn't 've been deeper than a foot.

(She makes her way to the folding stairs and points her flashlight down the stairs.)

And look at it now, not five minutes later. That's got to be at least three feet of water inching up the stairs.

SUGAR: That's a damn lie.

CAMILLE: A lie? See for yourself, you think I'm lying.

SUGAR: No, not the water, woman. I mean the way you constantly complain I snore in bed. Why you always insist on going around telling people I'm a snorer when you know perfectly well you've never heard a snore come out of me?

CAMILLE: I've never heard you snore? Sug, either you snore or we've got ourselves some giant toad lives under our bed and spends the whole night croaking at the moon.

SUGAR: Go on and make fun if you want, but I've never once—not in my entire life—heard any snoring coming out of me. And the slightest little peep escaped my lips at night, I'd be the first to hear it. You know what a light sleeper I am.

CAMILLE: Oh yeah, you a light sleeper, all right. In our bedroom downstairs five minutes ago, I'm wading through water in the pitch dark, like I'm in some kind of dream or something, shouting, "Sugar, Sugar, the house is flooding." And you know what you do, you light sleeper, you?

SUGAR (*shrugging*): Me? Why I jump right out of bed.

CAMILLE: No, that was just now—and only after I gave you a couple good whacks with my pillow to wake you up again. I tell you the house is filling up with water, I go splashing off down the hall with the flashlight to see if I can find where the water's coming from, and when I come back in the bedroom, what do I hear in the dark? That giant toad we got in there snoring his brains out again.

SUGAR: Now, Camille, you know I was up before dawn yesterday morning to see if the hurricane was still heading this way. Sure I'm a little sleepy tonight. What man wouldn't be after the day we had?

CAMILLE: But that's just it, Sugar. The rain's been over, I don't know, a good ten hours, maybe more. The hurricane's way up in Mississippi, Tennessee by now. So where's it from, all this water? It makes no sense.

SUGAR: How should I know where the water's coming from? *You* woke *me* up. I was sound asleep.

CAMILLE: You'd rather that I'd let you drown in bed?

SUGAR: All I'm saying is how am I supposed to know just where the hell it's coming from. Something sprung a leak, I guess.

CAMILLE: A leak? You really think our house is filled with water— our bedroom, kitchen, parlor, dining room—they're flooded thanks to . . . what? . . . some dripping pipe?

SUGAR: Might be the water heater or maybe something in the bathroom. You sure you jiggled the toilet handle before you went to bed?

CAMILLE: You think an overflowing toilet put all this water in our house?

SUGAR: I didn't say the toilet made it flood. It's just you never take the time to shake the handle when you're done. (*Brief pause.*)

And really, when you get right down to it, such a simple thing to do. Wouldn't take you half a second. And then you wonder why our bill's so high.

CAMILLE: Well, Sugar, they come to find out our toilet's why there's water everywhere, I guarantee our bill will run a little high next month.

SUGAR: All right, all right, it's probably not the toilet made it flood.

(*Pause.*)

But by the way, as long as you and I are talking water bills, did you remember it this month? The bill, I mean. I think it's due the first.

CAMILLE: We've got a house that's filling up with water. Every stick of furniture we own and everything electrical, every piece of clothing's ruined. The two of us could drown tonight. But none of that concerns my husband. No, the thing that worries him the most: maybe I might not mail a bill on time. He wouldn't want us both to drown and not have paid our water bill this month.

SUGAR: You always put off paying them, the bills. Then every month, we've got those fees to pay. The water bill this month, it's just exactly why I have to nag you all the time.

CAMILLE: It's just exactly why you have to be a nag? Because you knew the day would come when we'd be trapped, with water lapping at the attic stairs from God knows where, and I'd forget to bring the bill. And that's "exactly why" you always have to be a pain in the neck about it every month?

SUGAR: "Exactly" in the sense of something unexpected that would come along like this, and we'd be stuck up here without our things, and then you couldn't mail the bill on time.

CAMILLE: Well, maybe I should dive into the pool that used to be our dining room and try to fish you out the bill before it's late.

SUGAR: But what's the good in doing that? By now, the bill's too soggy for an envelope.

CAMILLE: Will you forget the water bill for two seconds and tell me where all this water's coming from? No leaking pipe could fill our house just since we went to bed tonight.

SUGAR: Depends how big a leak it is.

CAMILLE: We're talking three damn feet of water, Sug, not just some bathroom mat that's soaking wet. And anyway, the water wouldn't stay. Even if we had a leak inside, the house would drain, not fill up like a tub.

SUGAR: I didn't say it's leaking from a pipe. I said I didn't know where the water might be coming from.

(*Pause.*)

And nothing about it on the radio—what stations I could get, at least—before we went to bed tonight. Of course, the batteries were nearly dead. It was hard to hear them clear, the news reports.

CAMILLE: I don't suppose that it occurred to you to bring the radio with you when you came up here?

SUGAR: You didn't bring it up with you?

CAMILLE: No, I grabbed the flashlight. The radio was on your side of the bed.

SUGAR: You want the radio so bad, I'll go down right now and get it for you.

CAMILLE: Are you out of your mind, Sugar?

SUGAR: I've waded in water way deeper than that before.

CAMILLE: I'm not letting you down those stairs again.

(*Silence.*)

SUGAR: Should've said something, you wanted the radio up here.

CAMILLE: Didn't think I needed to, something as obvious as that.

SUGAR: Nothing's obvious when you got water rushing into your house in the middle of the night.

CAMILLE: Just what I was getting at before. The water's coming in the house from somewhere else.

SUGAR: Probably the city's pumps backed up. Or maybe one of them went down. A miracle they work at all as old's they are.

CAMILLE: You telling me one broken pump put all this water in our house?

SUGAR: It doesn't work like that. One goes bad, another's got to do the job of two. So it burns out. And then a third one goes, and then—

CAMILLE: Yeah, yeah, yeah. One after another they all give out—

SUGAR: Until it floods. That's how it works. That's how everything works down here. One piece fails, the whole thing falls apart.

CAMILLE: But that makes no sense.

SUGAR: Ain't that the truth.

CAMILLE: No, I mean it makes no sense the pumps are why it's flooding now. The time the sun went down tonight, the streets were clear. That young couple from around the block— Charlene and what's-his-name—they were out walking their dog, remember? There wasn't any standing water left. Even if the pumping stations all shut down, there wasn't nothing left for them to pump.

SUGAR: Then you tell me. What else could it be?

(*Silence.*)

CAMILLE: What if you were right before?

SUGAR: What about?

CAMILLE: About a leak.

SUGAR: So now it's you thinks our bathroom's where the flood is coming from?

CAMILLE: No, Sugar, it's not about our plumbing we need to worry. What if it's the levee giving way?

SUGAR: The levee? Oh, don't talk crazy, woman. The U.S. Army built those things. The U.S. Army Corps of Engineers. You think they don't know how to hold the water back? A levee's not just mud. There's steel inside. No way a storm like what we had today could breach a levee.

CAMILLE: Yeah, we dodged a bullet when it veered away from us.

SUGAR: Dodged a bullet? I told you we had nothing to worry about. Those hurricanes that come this way, they hit the mouth of the river and always veer off to the east.

CAMILLE: But you got to admit, it was bad enough this morning. Maybe all those people left town yesterday weren't such idiots after all, now were they, Sug?

SUGAR: That'll be the day I evacuate for some goddamn hurricane. We rode out Betsy when I was a boy, and I don't know how many other storms since. I'm not sitting twelve hours in a traffic jam from here to Baton Rouge just to wind up stuck in some motel in Houston for a hundred bucks a night. Not when you know the storm's gonna veer off anyway and hit Mississippi like it always does.

CAMILLE: Maybe so, but I'd 've been a whole lot happier today sitting on the foot of a bed in that hundred-dollar motel in Texas watching it all on the TV.

(*Pause.*)

I was scared this morning, Sugar, when the storm come through. The wind clawing at the roof the way it did, shaking all the windows, rooting underneath the door—it was like some kind of beast battering the house, looking for a way in, a way to get at you and me.

SUGAR: Hell, I been through worse weather fishing down at Delacroix Island. A squall sneaks up behind you out there and day turns into night—now that'll put the fear of God in you, especially if your engine won't crank the first time you give the starter a tug or two.

CAMILLE: I hate it when you go out there all alone in that little boat of yours.

SUGAR: A day like that and things go bad, another man wouldn't be the slightest bit of help—just someone else to drown with me and feed the crabs.

CAMILLE: Don't talk like that. You love to frighten me.

SUGAR: Come on, Camille, with all the fishing trips I've made alone, how many times I ever come home drowned?

CAMILLE: You think you're cute, but what's going on tonight, it's nothing to joke about. I couldn't say for sure—too hard to tell with the streetlights out and the moon behind a cloud—but when I pulled the bedroom curtain back, it looked like a river running wild outside, the water swirling over everything out there.

SUGAR: Well, no surprise in that. Makes sense, in fact. Maybe it's a water main outside that burst. Or sewers backing up from all the rain.

CAMILLE: A sewer backing up wouldn't put three feet of water in our house. It has to be the levees, Sug.

SUGAR: Camille, we got to be twelve, fifteen blocks from the levee. You have any idea how much it would take to flood the streets from there to here and then fill up our house with water three feet deep?

CAMILLE (*checking the water from the staircase opening*): Four feet deep. It's come up another foot, at least.

SUGAR: Then four feet deep. Woman, you talking more water than you know.

CAMILLE: But that's exactly what I'm saying. Where else could so much water be coming from, it's not some levee giving way? That's Lake Pontchartrain down there in our living room, I guarantee.

SUGAR: So maybe it is the levees. I don't know.

(*Silence.*)

And anyway, what difference does it make where the hell it's coming from?

CAMILLE: We need to know what we are dealing with.

SUGAR: I'll tell you what we're dealing with—water, plain and simple.

(*He joins CAMILLE and points his flashlight down the stairs.*)

Lots and lots of water.

(*Silence.*)

Anyway, maybe you ought to stop worrying about what exactly
happened and start worrying about what we're gonna do now
we're up here.

CAMILLE: And what do *you* propose that we should do?

SUGAR: Wait until the water falls, I guess.

CAMILLE: What makes you think the water will go down? The land
around here's nine, ten feet below sea level. There's nowhere
lower it can run off to. And for all we know, the whole city may
be flooding this very minute.

SUGAR: That's just plain foolishness to say a thing like that. Why
would the city flood? The hurricane's long gone.

CAMILLE: Exactly. Something else is going on.

SUGAR: What are you getting at, Camille? You think the city's
gonna sink tonight, and we all drown? If you were right,
imagine what that would mean: a city under water. It's insane.

CAMILLE: You never heard of Atlantis?

SUGAR: A fairy tale for children, that's all Atlantis was. It's crazy
what you saying, woman.

CAMILLE: Crazy? Things only sound crazy until they happen. But
once they do, then people want to know why no one saw it
coming, what went wrong.

SUGAR: New Orleans has been here for—what's it been?—three
hundred years? You really think tonight's the night the city dies?

CAMILLE: I wish I knew why you're so sure it won't be tonight New
Orleans disappears.

SUGAR: You hear yourself? New Orleans disappear? You act like
this is Noah and the Flood we're dealing with. A little water in
our house, that's all we're talking. A couple hours, it'll start to
drain. You'll see.

(*Lights fade.*)

(*Lights rise. An hour later. CAMILLE is sitting on a box. SUGAR is distracting himself by rooting around in the things stored in the attic.*)

SUGAR: What's all this junk we've stored up here?

CAMILLE: Think I know? Toys. Old furniture. What difference does it make? Five feet of water—most likely even more than that by now—is sitting in our house this very minute. Everything we own is gone, destroyed.

SUGAR: Not everything. This stuff is all OK. And nothing we can do about downstairs. So tell me what exactly we've got here.

CAMILLE: The things you wouldn't let me throw away.

SUGAR: You mean the things we thought we'd need again.

CAMILLE (*turning toward the attic stairs*): The water, Sugar, the water's everywhere.

SUGAR (*picking up a toy beside him to distract her*): Like memories, sort of, stored away, these things.

CAMILLE: Yeah, like you said, just so much useless junk.

SUGAR: What's in that trunk? Your hope chest, isn't it?

CAMILLE: That's what my mother called it, anyway.

SUGAR: What hopes are lurking in that chest of yours?

CAMILLE: I don't remember. Photographs, I guess. And souvenirs. You know, just sentimental stuff you put away and never think about again.

SUGAR: Let's see.

(*Opens the trunk, roots around a bit, pulls out a wedding dress, and holds it up against himself.*)

Remember?

CAMILLE: Yeah, you made a lovely bride. (*Pause.*) Give it here.

(*Taking the dress from him and covering herself with it.*)

SUGAR (*looking at a wedding album from the trunk*): All morning long, the rain kept coming down.

CAMILLE: My father told me how it was good luck, to have it raining on your wedding day. And everyone was sure the rain would stop at least in time for us to go to church.

SUGAR: Except, as it turned out, they all were wrong.

CAMILLE: It rained so loud no one could hear the priest, and when we kissed, the thunder made us jump.

SUGAR: How many times I got to tell you there wasn't any thunder at the end?

CAMILLE: Yeah, I know. There was no clap of thunder. Just your heart, exploding with undying love for me.

SUGAR: At least that's how it felt when I kissed you.

CAMILLE: I've heard you tell that joke for over thirty years.

SUGAR: It's not a joke. How can you call it that? Exaggeration, maybe. But not much.

CAMILLE: I didn't mean to hurt your feelings, Sug. You know I think it's sweet when you say that.

SUGAR: I really was afraid my heart would burst. You looked so lovely standing there in white, your veil thrown back, your eyes about to close. I guess I couldn't quite believe my luck.

CAMILLE: You mean to have a girl like me love you?

SUGAR: More like . . . to find a girl like you to love.

CAMILLE: It wasn't 'cause I loved you half to death?

SUGAR: Oh sure. I liked the way you looked at me. But even more than that, I guess I knew I needed someone I could love. Someone like you.

CAMILLE: *Like* me? You mean you could have loved somebody else?

SUGAR: Aw, honey, you know that never crossed my mind. I wanted you.

CAMILLE: Still, as far as you're concerned, I didn't have to be the one you married, did I? Another girl would've done you just as well.

SUGAR: It's not a question of you or someone else. I was—what?— twenty-three, twenty-four when we got married. I just didn't see the point in being single anymore. I needed a reason to straighten out, you know, to get up every morning and go to work, not to come home fall-down-drunk from all those bars on Chef Menteur every night. I needed something to stop me living the way I was living in those days. (*Pause.*) You know, a wife.

CAMILLE: Well, that's about the most romantic thing I ever heard.

(*She throws the dress over his head.*)

You mean I was nothing but a cure for your hangover.

SUGAR: No, of course not.

(*Thinking it over, as he hangs the dress up on a rafter.*)

But, yeah, in a way, you healed me.

CAMILLE: Healed you? Of what?

SUGAR: Of being me. Of being what I was.

CAMILLE: But that's the boy I fell in love with.

SUGAR: Maybe so. But you wouldn't 've liked being that boy's wife, I promise you.

CAMILLE: How you know what I'd like?

SUGAR: C'mon, darling, you weren't nothing but a convent-school girl back then in that little plaid skirt you used to wear. What were you, seventeen years old, when I met you?

CAMILLE: Nearly eighteen. But I knew what I was getting into with a boy like you.

(Pause.)

And so did my daddy.

SUGAR: Damn, he hated me at first, didn't he? And what did I ever do to him?

CAMILLE: Fell in love with me, that's what.

SUGAR: Or even worse, made you fall in love with me.

CAMILLE: Yeah, that's something he never could forgive you for.

(Silence.)

Didn't much care for your name, neither. "Sugar? What kind of name is Sugar for a man?" he used to say. "Sounds like a horse's name, a name like that."

SUGAR: Your mama, though, she liked me from the start.

CAMILLE: They were worried about different things, those two.

SUGAR: I guess we know how that goes, huh?

(Pause.)

CAMILLE: This isn't the night to get into all of that again.

SUGAR: No, you right. We got other things to worry about right now.

(Pause.)

Like how damn hot it is. It's sweltering up here, isn't it?

CAMILLE: Yeah, it's some hot. I can barely stand it.

SUGAR: I think it's kind of cozy, you and me up here alone.

CAMILLE *(fanning herself with something she's found)*: I'm dying. Must be a hundred degrees at least.

SUGAR: Try to think of something else, Camille.

CAMILLE: Then why don't you tell me one of your stories, Sug, like you used to do when we first met?

SUGAR: What kind of story?

CAMILLE: I don't care. Something scary, something to make me
   shiver and cool me off.

SUGAR: My daddy told me a ghost story once.

CAMILLE: You never told me any ghost story before.

SUGAR: It's too sad. I never thought you'd want to hear it, sad as it is.

CAMILLE: Well, if ever there was a night for sad stories, Sugar,
   this is it.

SUGAR: Yeah, you right about that.

CAMILLE (*settling sideways onto a rocking horse*): So how's it go,
   this ghost story of yours?

SUGAR: There was this freighter three days out of New Orleans,
   loaded with cotton and on its way to Panama. They're out
   there in the middle of the Gulf when the wife and the daughter
   of the ship's captain both die, a couple hours apart, of this
   fever they'd had since their first day at sea.

CAMILLE: Mother and daughter both?

SUGAR: I told you it was a sad story. The old-timers, they tell the
   younger hands it was all his own fault, the captain. Bad luck to
   bring a woman aboard a boat.

CAMILLE: Some old myth or something?

SUGAR (*looking at her as if she's simpleminded*): Just good sense,
   that. You put a woman on a ship and the men fall to fighting
   over her, everybody'd wind up dead or drowned long before
   they ever make it back to port again. So it was only as a special
   birthday present to his little girl, the captain taking her on a
   run like that. "Damn fool couldn't deny her anything," that's
   the way Daddy explained it. But mother and child, they both
   get sick their first day out, while the ship is still nosing down
   the Mississippi. Probably just seasickness, the captain tells
   himself—

CAMILLE: But you don't get fever from that.

SUGAR: And you don't get seasick on a river where you got
   shoreline on both banks to keep you steady. So after a while,
   he sends the second mate to see to them. The sailor tends the
   woman and the girl best he can, but when they get too weak

to swallow the aspirins he's taken from the medicine locker, all he can do is crush the pills under his thumb in the bowl of a spoon and add a few drops of water so they can drink the medicine. It doesn't do any good, though.

CAMILLE: The poor captain.

SUGAR: They wrap the bodies in canvas and bury them at sea. It's the custom for the ship's navigator to shoot the sun and fix the spot where the bodies are slipped over the side, so he notes it on the ship's chart and brings it to the captain for entry in the log.

CAMILLE: Why would anybody care? It's not as if you could put up a memorial out there in the middle of the ocean.

SUGAR: I guess it's just too sad the other way, abandoning the dead to an unmarked grave, even if it is the sea. Anyway, the freighter makes port in Colón and offloads its cotton bales and takes on its cargo, probably coffee, then retraces its route back home.

CAMILLE: The captain must have been a hard man to survive the loss of his whole family.

SUGAR: Not hard enough for what happened next. Two days out of Panama on their way back to New Orleans, an officer calls the captain to the bridge. Fifty yards off the starboard bow, the water has risen up—

CAMILLE: Risen up? You mean a wave?

SUGAR: No, the water rises up in the shape of two figures—one a bit taller than the other—and just sort of hangs there in the air. The captain drops his binoculars. "Sir," the navigator whispers, "we're very close to the spot, very close."

CAMILLE: Oh, you making this all up.

SUGAR: It's my father's story, not mine. As the ship slides past, the figures tremble there in the sunlight. Finally, the watch sees the two columns of water collapse after the stern has passed them by.

CAMILLE: What does the captain do?

SUGAR: By the time the ship docks a few days later in New Orleans, the captain's been locked in his cabin. Two orderlies from De Paul's lead him down the gangplank in a straitjacket.

CAMILLE: Now who'd believe a story like that?

SUGAR: Well, even being a boy, I didn't believe him yet, either. So Daddy tells me the rest. In a big port town like New Orleans, with boats coming and going every day, a story like that gets around in a hurry. So when the ship sets sail again a week later on the same run, the old newspaper, the *Item,* it sends a photographer along.

CAMILLE: And what happens when they pass the spot?

SUGAR: Same thing. These two watery figures rise up and shimmer there in the sunlight until the ship passes by. The paper, the *Item,* it runs the photo on the front page, and by the end of the week, the seafarers' union is threatening to strike, the shipping lines don't change the route to Panama. (*Pause.*) You know, they got that photograph—the picture of those two columns of water, the one that ran in the paper—they got it in some kind of archives on the third floor of the main library down on Tulane Avenue.

(*Silence.*)

CAMILLE: So did they?

SUGAR: Did they what?

CAMILLE: Did they change the route to Panama?

SUGAR: Hell yeah. The owners of the four shipping lines out of New Orleans, they had dinner that Sunday afternoon in one of those private dining rooms on the second floor of Antoine's. While they're sipping their coffee, waiting for the baked Alaska to come out, they take a napkin and plot a new course for their ships. Daddy said they still got that napkin in one of those display cases at the restaurant. And it's a fact the new route they plotted at lunch that day has been followed ever since.

CAMILLE: And no one ever went out there again? I mean where the woman and her little girl were buried.

SUGAR: In all that time, more'n fifty years now, no ship has passed within ten miles of the spot. So whether the sea is calm there or whether a mother and her daughter have risen up like pillars of water every day since, no one can say.

(*Silence.*)

CAMILLE (*shuddering*): Even hot as it is right now, it gives me goose bumps, thinking of that woman and her baby waiting out there in the middle of the ocean all alone.

SUGAR: Waiting for what? That's what I don't understand. What were they looking for?

CAMILLE: You think the dead don't have a claim on us?

SUGAR: Yeah, sure they do. But what is it they want, the dead?

CAMILLE: Whatever it is we haven't got to give 'em.

SUGAR: Man, the things scare you witless when you small, they just make you sad when you get old, don't they?

(*Silence.*)

CAMILLE: Well, it's a good story, but I'm still hot.

SUGAR: All the heat gets trapped up here.

CAMILLE: Come noon, this attic's gonna turn into an oven.

SUGAR: We'll be out of here long before then.

CAMILLE: What makes you think so?

SUGAR (*checking the depth of the water at the stairs*): Come see. It's better, isn't it? Not quite so deep.

CAMILLE (*joining him and pointing her flashlight down the hole*): No, the water is still coming up.

SUGAR: But don't you think it's slowing down, at least?

CAMILLE: Four steps were dry last time I looked, and now there's only three that I can see. That doesn't look like "slowing down" to me.

SUGAR: Well maybe it's not done yet coming up. But how much longer can it flood like this?

CAMILLE: Until the water finds its level. Lake Pontchartrain's a few hundred square miles of water on a normal day. You add Katrina, no telling how deep it's gonna get before it stops.

SUGAR: I can't believe the levees failed.

CAMILLE: You think it's more than one?

SUGAR: I don't know, but why would one collapse and not the others? Those levees, they're all made the same. It makes no sense. The Corps of Engineers have promised beaucoup times the levees they'd hold against a Category 3. Katrina couldn't have been any more than that. The time she got here, after crossing Plaquemines and St. Bernard, how much of her could there've been left? We've had winds as bad before.

CAMILLE: And more rain. Remember that flood in May ten years ago? Just a summer rainstorm, but the city got twenty inches in eight hours. And still it didn't flood half as bad as this.

SUGAR: Maybe it's not the lake. Maybe something else went wrong that we don't know about.

CAMILLE: Like what?

SUGAR: Could be a ship or barge broke loose from its moorings in the Mississippi. Punched a hole in those river levees up near the zoo or along the French Quarter somewhere. Or could be something else we're overlooking. I don't know where it's coming from, all this water. But maybe we'd be smart to find a way up on the roof in case we need to get there later on.

CAMILLE: You think the water will get as high as that?

SUGAR: No, probably not. Still, just to be on the safe side, we ought to look around up here for tools, something I could use to cut our way out of here we need to. Wouldn't hurt to find some food as well, or maybe something we could drink.

CAMILLE: Good idea. About the tools, I mean. If ever there was any food up here, though, the roaches would have feasted on it long ago.

SUGAR: Yeah, but you never know what you're gonna find once you start looking.

CAMILLE (*turning away to search another part of the attic*): Then be careful what you look for, Sugar. There's usually a good reason things get hidden.

SUGAR (*putting on a bull's head mask from a box and turning to CAMILLE with his flashlight on his mask from below*): Hey, look at this.

(*CAMILLE turns and laughs.*)

I found a box of our old costumes left from Mardi Gras.

(*He brings a sexy feathered mask from the box to CAMILLE.*)

Here.

CAMILLE (*putting on the mask*): It's been a long time since we went in masks to Carnival.

SUGAR (*turning his light on her mask*): I don't know what it is, but there's something about a woman in a mask I've always liked.

CAMILLE: Well, there's something about wearing a mask sets a woman free.

SUGAR: You thinking of that Mardi Gras before we married?

CAMILLE: You imagine I might forget that night?

SUGAR: We were so drunk.

CAMILLE: Not half as drunk as we pretended.

SUGAR: Where was it?

CAMILLE: Your uncle's house.

SUGAR: My uncle's? No, it was Emelda's place, wasn't it? Not Uncle Duncan's.

CAMILLE: Sure it was your uncle's. Just off Prytania. That big white house.

SUGAR: Yeah, that's right.

CAMILLE: We walked there after the parades when the rain began to fall. It was getting cold all afternoon, remember?

SUGAR: You started trembling in that flimsy costume you were wearing. You went as—what was it?

CAMILLE (*veiling the bottom of her face with the back of her hand*): A harem girl.

SUGAR: Yeah, yeah. That was quite an outfit that you made.

CAMILLE: My father, he threw a fit that morning when he saw me in it. But Mama reminded him I was already engaged. She said the only thing mattered was whether you approved.

SUGAR: Oh, I approved all right.

CAMILLE: I found out later just how much you did.

SUGAR: We had to get you warm somehow. I didn't want you catching cold.

CAMILLE: But how'd we wind up in that bedroom with your uncle downstairs?

SUGAR: You don't remember? He left us in the house all alone and told us lock the door behind us when we were done changing into something warm.

CAMILLE: Oh yeah. He had a party in the Quarter he was late for. (*Pause.*) Your family never guessed that he was gay?

SUGAR: Sure they knew. Just no one ever said. Mardi Gras wasn't the only day people went around in masks back then.

CAMILLE: I tell you, I look in the mirror these days, sometimes I think it's a mask staring back at me. (*She touches her cheek.*) How'd this face get old so fast? 'Cause underneath it, I feel just the same I always did.

SUGAR: You don't look old behind that mask you got on now.

CAMILLE: Then shall I keep it on for you?

SUGAR (*laughing*): Think I don't remember that? You lying naked on Uncle Duncan's bed—with just that square of yellow silk across your face.

CAMILLE: I wouldn't have had the nerve without my mask. It let me play that I was some harem girl called against my will to be your concubine.

SUGAR: Where'd you ever learn a word like that?

CAMILLE: The nuns at school. It's somewhere in the Bible.

SUGAR: You looked at me when I came in and whispered, "Shall I keep it on for you, my mask?" I'll tell you, we came pretty close that night.

CAMILLE: But you were such a gentleman. Too much the gentleman, as far as I was concerned.

SUGAR: I thought that's how you showed a girl respect.

CAMILLE: It wasn't respect I was looking for just then.

SUGAR: It gets to be a habit in a hurry, don't it, the way you treat a person that you love? And so you never see when she's asking something different than you're used to giving.

CAMILLE (*teasing*): I think maybe you were just too scared of what my daddy would've done, he'd found out I'd been your concubine.

SUGAR: Scared of your daddy? Me? No way. (*Pause.*) But disappointing your mama, that I wouldn't 've liked.

CAMILLE: Yeah, I miss her, too.

SUGAR: She was some sweet, that woman.

CAMILLE: Loved you more than she loved me, I think.

SUGAR: Only 'cause she knew how much I loved her daughter.

CAMILLE: You flirtin' with me?

SUGAR: It's that mask you wearing. (*Taking off his shirt.*) Take off your gown, Camille.

CAMILLE: What, here? Tonight? With water rushing up the stairs? Are you out of your mind?

SUGAR: Why not? You got something better else to do? Let's go back to that night at Uncle Duncan's house. You leave on nothing but your mask, and I promise this time I won't be such a gentleman.

CAMILLE: Where would we even—

SUGAR: Right here. On your hope chest.

CAMILLE: With all that water coming up the stairs?

SUGAR: We might not have another chance.

CAMILLE: You said we'd be all right up here.

SUGAR: We'll be fine, I promise you.

(*He takes the wedding dress and spreads it over the chest like a sheet.*)

Let's go back to the beginning, Camille. We're in Uncle
Duncan's bedroom up the stairs. The windows are all fogged
up with rain. There's not much light. The room is full of
shadows. And you, you're wearing nothing but a mask.

CAMILLE: Sug, this isn't the time for foolishness like that. The
world outside is being washed away.

SUGAR: Maybe it's not the end of the world that's going on outside.
Maybe it could be for us a new world just beginning.

CAMILLE: You talking crazy.

(*Taking off her mask and handing it back to him along with his
shirt that she's picked up.*)

Put your shirt back on, old man. And put away this foolish
mask.

SUGAR (*still shirtless, but taking off his mask if it's still on at this
point*): Camille, we may not get another chance.

CAMILLE (*more gently, as she folds the wedding dress and puts it
away*): Sugar, put your shirt back on. We wouldn't want you
catching cold.

(*Lights fade.*)

(*Lights rise. Another hour later. CAMILLE is huddled in a corner of the attic, dozing. SUGAR is stretched out on the floor, snoring loudly.*)

CAMILLE (*startled awake by SUGAR's snoring*): Sug? Sugar. Wake up. We fell asleep again.

SUGAR (*shaken awake by CAMILLE*): What? What's wrong?

CAMILLE: You were sleeping.

SUGAR (*half awake*): Sleeping? Me? No, you crazy, woman. I'm wide awake. I was just resting my eyes is all.

(*He sits up and stretches, yawning loudly.*)

The water start to go down yet?

CAMILLE (*checking the stairs*): Oh God, it's up another foot at least. Maybe more. What will we do if it keeps rising?

SUGAR (*joining her at the stairs*): I don't know. But even if it stays right where it's at, nobody knows we're in here. The sun come up tomorrow morning and the water hasn't fallen yet, as hot as it already is, this attic's gonna roast us to a crisp.

CAMILLE: Forget tomorrow morning. What are people doing tonight, Sugar, the ones who can't get in their attics like we did?

SUGAR: Standing on their chairs by now, I guess, climbing up on tables, countertops.

CAMILLE: But how long can they last like that, alone in the dark, water up around their throats?

SUGAR: You'd be surprised what people can survive when there's no other choice that's left to them. A lady down in St. Bernard, she stood three days on a kitchen chair when Betsy flooded everything out east.

CAMILLE: And she survived?

SUGAR: Oh yeah, she made it through till somebody heard her screaming there. They said her legs by then were swollen up the size of an elephant's. But she survived.

CAMILLE: If the water keeps on rising, Sugar? If it gets up ceiling high?

SUGAR: It can't go on all night.

CAMILLE: But if it does?

SUGAR (*turning away from the stairs*): It gets that high, a kitchen chair won't be enough.

CAMILLE (*following him*): But wait a minute, Sugar. If inside water's six feet deep already, then, Jesus, it must be eight feet in the street. Our place is raised, but what about Miss Jeanfreau's house next door? It's on a slab. A slab house, it's only eight feet to the ceiling from the floor.

SUGAR: But Miss Jeanfreau, she's got an attic. Remember? She asked me go up there last winter and light her heater. I'm sure she's safe up there by now.

CAMILLE: Oh, Sugar, the woman's seventy-five years old. And she can't walk without a cane.

SUGAR: I'm sure she's fine.

(*Silence.*)

CAMILLE: Who could bear to think of such a thing? Miss Jeanfreau, all those people in pitch-dark rooms, balanced on a chair, a coffee table, standing on their mattresses with water up around their mouths—old people, parents holding up their kids against the ceiling—can you imagine what's going on right now? It's unbelievable. How many lives, one by one, are being lost this very minute? Here, in New Orleans, in our own city. How many men, how many women, how many children—children, Sugar—trapped in rooms so dark they can't even see the water drowning them?

SUGAR: But we don't know for sure what's going on. We have to keep our spirits up, Camille. Divert ourselves. Think of something else.

CAMILLE: It's horrible the things will happen here, the water keeps on coming up tonight.

SUGAR: Whatever happens, we've got to trust it's all God's will.

CAMILLE: So it's God's will those little children drown, the cripples in wheelchairs, the folks too old to climb their attic stairs?

SUGAR: It's not for us to understand. It's a night to put our trust in faith.

CAMILLE: That would take more faith than I've got left.

(*Long silence.*)

SUGAR: Listen, did you hear that? Shouts, I think, or screams.

CAMILLE: No, nothing. I didn't hear a thing.

SUGAR (*goes to the stairs and cranes his neck to hear better*): Are you sure? I thought I heard something.

CAMILLE (*joins SUGAR at the stairs*): Just the water sloshing against the house, most likely. Or maybe a cat up a tree.

(*Silence.*)

Nobody's coming for us, Sug.

SUGAR (*turning away from the stairs*): Then we'll just have to put our trust in God to get us through this.

CAMILLE (*still staring down the stairs*): You mean the God that's drowning all those innocent people tonight.

SUGAR: If He didn't test our faith, it wouldn't grow, our trust in Providence.

CAMILLE (*crossing from the stairs*): Providence? There's a good eight feet of water in the street. You think God is getting ready to send his angels down here to fly through the city and carry us all off to high ground? You think that's what's going on outside right now?

SUGAR: Don't blaspheme, Camille.

CAMILLE: You know, a sky full of angels saving the faithful. Listen. You can hear their wings fluttering in the dark. In fact, that's probably what you heard just now—angels hovering in the night, coming to save us all from a watery grave.

SUGAR: Mock all you want, if ever there was a night for faith, this is it.

CAMILLE: If ever there was a night to question your religion, this is it. How can you worship a god who'd do this to us?

SUGAR: Oh, don't talk foolish, woman. You think it's God did this to us. This water is probably just somebody didn't do his job. Some terrible mistake somebody made and didn't care enough to set it right.

CAMILLE: Then that's even worse than God did this to us. You and me, we've lost everything we own. How many people drowned in their own bedrooms since the sun went down? And it's all because somebody cut some corners, didn't pay attention to some detail, decided things were close enough to right and let it go at that? You telling me that's why we're trapped here in our own attic in the middle of the night with water lapping at the stairs? That's the reason we could die tonight, you and me?

SUGAR: If it's our levees broke, they didn't fall down all by themselves, Camille. If it's the levees giving way, there's somebody responsible.

CAMILLE: Well, if it's not God responsible, then the men did this to us, I hope they never lie down in bed they don't hear the ghosts of those they drowned tonight crying out for help. I die tonight, I'll never let them sleep, those murderers, I promise you.

(*Long silence.*)

SUGAR: We're not going to die. Not if we find a way out onto the roof.

(*Silence.*)

We need something sharp. Or maybe something we could use to pry the boards loose. (*He looks around.*) If I could just work that vent free over there, we wouldn't have to cut a thing. Slip out through the hole instead.

CAMILLE: Can you knock it free?

SUGAR: The screws in its base must be loose. It rattles whenever the wind blows hard.

CAMILLE: So that's the thing we always hear at night?

SUGAR: See you can't find something back there I could use like a screwdriver.

CAMILLE (*searching through some boxes in the back of the attic*): There's nothing here.

SUGAR (*also searching the attic*): Now watch where you step in the dark over there. The floor is soft in spots.

CAMILLE: Where?

SUGAR: Everywhere up here we don't have flooring. It's nothing but sheetrock between the joists. You'll fall right through the ceiling, you put your weight in the wrong place.

CAMILLE: You mean I could fall through the ceiling and drown?

SUGAR: Just be careful where you step. (*Pause.*) Isn't that Frankie's toy toolbox?

CAMILLE: Where?

SUGAR: There . . . behind that table lamp.

CAMILLE: It is. It's Frankie's toys.

SUGAR: What's he got there in his tool kit? A screwdriver, maybe?

CAMILLE: Yeah, but tiny.

(*She holds it up.*)

SUGAR: Don't worry. That'll do.

(*He takes the screwdriver.*)

CAMILLE: And look, his baseball cap.

SUGAR (*starting to slowly unscrew the vent in the roof with the little screwdriver*): It barely fits, but it'll do. The screw is turning. (*Grunting with effort.*) Slowly, but it's turning.

CAMILLE (*handling a child's baseball cap*): Remember how he wore this thing twenty-four hours a day when he was small? Wouldn't even take it off long enough for me to wash it. I'd have to wait until he was sound asleep before I could ease it off his head at night.

SUGAR (*working on the vent*): Yeah, and remember the afternoon he lost it at the picture show? The way he cried, you'd 've thought the world was ending.

CAMILLE: It took five minutes just to calm him down enough to get him to tell us what was wrong.

SUGAR: And then we had to go back in again to find his hat.

CAMILLE: You on your hands and knees in the dark, crawling behind the row that we'd been sitting in.

SUGAR: Reaching underneath the seats, searching for his hat—

CAMILLE: Until you grabbed that woman's ankle in the dark.

SUGAR: Good thing his cap was underneath there, too.

CAMILLE: Her, screaming like a rat had bit her leg or something.

SUGAR: Me, crawling backwards out of there, waving the cap over my head, whispering like a crazy person, "I was looking for a hat, I was looking for a hat."

(*Silence.*)

CAMILLE: The things you do, you got a child.

SUGAR: The things you should have done.

CAMILLE: Not tonight, Sug. We're not talking about all that tonight.

SUGAR (*having trouble with the vent and turning to her*): What did we ever do to him, made the boy so angry?

CAMILLE: I used to think it was us responsible, too. But now I'm not so sure.

SUGAR (*stops working on the vent and turns to CAMILLE*): How could it not be the parents' fault, things turn out the way they did?

CAMILLE: You think it's all your parents' doing, you turned out the way you did?

SUGAR: I think the way I treated Frankie, it wasn't so different from how my father treated me.

CAMILLE: That boy adored you, he was small.

SUGAR: And I was small, I thought my daddy hung the moon.

CAMILLE: A father can only do what he thinks he ought to do.

SUGAR: That don't absolve him, things go wrong.

(*Silence.*)

CAMILLE: Maybe it's just plain easier for us to imagine we're the ones responsible. It would be a whole lot worse thinking that what's wrong with Frankie he never can outgrow.

SUGAR: I outgrew the life I lived when I was young.

CAMILLE: You never took up the habits Frankie's got.

SUGAR: Only 'cause you came along in time.

(*Silence.*)

CAMILLE: People think it's up to them, how their lives turn out. But when you get right down to it, how much luck—how much blind luck—decides which one of us gets to laugh and which one cries?

SUGAR: (*He tries to go back to work on the vent.*) Well, we could use some luck tonight, I'll tell you that.

CAMILLE: Compared to some tonight, we've maybe had our share of luck already.

SUGAR (*working on the vent with difficulty*): Then I think we need a second helping.

CAMILLE: You having trouble?

SUGAR (*giving up on the vent in exasperation*): My hands are too damn big for this toy screwdriver.

CAMILLE: Let me try.

SUGAR: I loosened all the screws. It shouldn't be too hard to do.

CAMILLE (*unscrewing the vent*): They're coming easy.

SUGAR: I'm starving. You sure there's nothing here to eat?

CAMILLE (*unscrewing the vent*): The roaches would have found it long ago.

SUGAR: Not if it's inside something sealed up tight.

CAMILLE (*unscrewing the vent*): I wouldn't have stored any food up here.

SUGAR: I'm talking just by accident. You know, something you might put up here by mistake, thinking it was something else.

CAMILLE (*unscrewing the vent*): Don't waste your time looking. I swear there's nothing here to find. Come hold your light so I can see the screws. I think the vent is nearly free.

SUGAR (*shining his light on the vent*): You're almost there. Just another turn or two.

CAMILLE (*loosening the vent*): I think I got it, Sugar. The vent's come loose.

SUGAR: Wait, let me see.

(*SUGAR struggles with the vent until it gives way. Moonlight streams in through the hole.*)

Yeah, it's free.

CAMILLE: Oh, thank God.

SUGAR: Let's get you on the roof.

(*They move the hope chest beneath the vent.*)

A boat comes by, and no one's there to call for help, they'll just go on and won't come back till who knows when.

(*SUGAR helps CAMILLE up onto the chest.*)

CAMILLE (*on the hope chest beneath the hole*): You coming, too,
    aren't you?
SUGAR: Yeah, right behind you. Just let me check how high the
    water is.

(*SUGAR goes to the stairs.*)

CAMILLE: How deep is it?
SUGAR (*dips his hand into the water and lifts it up dripping wet*):
    It's bad, real bad. Nearly in the attic now. It's time we got up on
    the roof.

(*SUGAR crosses to the chest.*)

CAMILLE: We'll be all right, won't we, Sug? Once we're on the roof,
    we'll be all right?
SUGAR (*as he begins to lift CAMILLE through the hole*): Woman,
    after what we been through and survived tonight, how could
    things get any worse?

(*Blackout.*)

ACT II

SCENE 1

(*The dark roof of the house in moonlight. The sound of water sloshing. CAMILLE begins to emerge from the hole where the vent had been.*)

CAMILLE (*with only her head out, surveying the scene in wonder*): Oh, Sugar, you won't believe the way it looks out here.

(*Silence.*)

Boost me up.

(*She climbs out of the hole and onto the roof, regarding what she sees in silence.*)

The water stretches off to the horizon. There's nothing but roofs and treetops left.

(*Silence.*)

They look like boats floating on the water, the roofs. Like some wrecked fleet of ships, all upside down, adrift in the middle of the ocean.

SUGAR (*unseen in the attic*): Anyone else made it to a roof?

CAMILLE: No one I can see from here. And not a single light, as far as I can tell. Even with the moon out, I've never seen a place as dark as this.

SUGAR (*unseen in the attic*): Shout and see anyone answers back.
CAMILLE (*shouting*): Anyone there?

(*Silence.*)

Anybody hear my voice?

(*Silence.*)

SUGAR (*unseen in the attic*): Someone answer?
CAMILLE: No one. It's deadly quiet out here, Sugar. Nothing but
the sound of water lapping at the roof.

(*Silence.*)

No dogs, no motors, no human voices. Nothing.
SUGAR (*unseen in the attic*): Try again.
CAMILLE (*shouting*): Hello? Hello?

(*Silence.*)

Anybody there?

(*Silence.*)

Miss Jeanfreau? Anybody?

(*Silence.*)

SUGAR (*unseen in the attic*): Any luck?
CAMILLE: Not a sound. No wind. No birds. Nobody knocking.
Nothing but the sloshing of the water.
SUGAR (*unseen in the attic*): Everyone's probably still sitting in
their attics, waiting for dawn before they get up on their roofs.
CAMILLE: The ones made it to their attics, maybe. But how many
people you think already drowned in all this water?

(*Silence.*)

Sugar, come up here. I'm frightened to be alone the way it is.

(*Silence.*)

It's all so still, so dark, so quiet. As if it's me alone survived what's happened.

SUGAR (*sticking his head through the vent hole*): You're not alone. I'm right here beside you. (*Pausing as he looks around.*) Jesus God.

(*Silence.*)

CAMILLE: Come up here on the roof with me.

SUGAR (*with only his head visible*): This hole is smaller than I thought it was.

(*Struggling to squeeze through.*)

I don't know if I can squeeze my body through.

(*Still struggling.*)

It's tight, this opening.

(*Wincing.*)

And sharp.

CAMILLE: Come on, Sugar. If I could do it, you can, too.

SUGAR (*trying to squeeze through*): No, the hole's too small for me.

CAMILLE: You'll fit. Just squeeze your shoulders like I did.

SUGAR (*apparently stuck*): I tell you it won't work, Camille.

CAMILLE: Then make the hole wider.

SUGAR (*with just his head and one arm visible*): With what? All I've
    got me are those toy tools of Frankie's.
CAMILLE: I'm not staying out here by myself, Sugar. You got to
    find a way to get up here.
SUGAR: Hang on a minute. Let me see what I can find to widen this.

(*He descends back into the attic.*)

CAMILLE (*shouting down the hole*): You need some help? I'll come
    back in.
SUGAR (*his head emerging through the hole*): No, you stay up here,
    no matter what. A boat comes by, and there isn't one of us to
    flag it down, we'll miss our chance. We'll just keep talking, you
    and me, until help comes. They must be on their way by now,
    the rescue boats and helicopters.
CAMILLE: I'd like it better you were here with me up on the roof.
SUGAR (*laughing with only his head visible*): I'm here with you—
    just not all of me. (*Pausing as he looks around.*) My God, it's
    beautiful though.
CAMILLE: What is?
SUGAR (*with only his head visible*): The moonlight on the water.
CAMILLE: And so, so still. I haven't heard another sound—no
    breeze, no animals, no baby crying in the dark. It frightens me
    for it to be so quiet.
SUGAR: The people, they'll come out when there's some light.
    They're huddled in their attics now. The roofs are just too thick
    for us to hear them there.
CAMILLE: That must be it. We're surely not the only ones who
    made it through all this.

(*Silence.*)

SUGAR: I'd forgotten what it's like before the sun comes up. How
    calm, how peaceful everything can seem.

CAMILLE (*sitting*): I don't know you and I ever watched a dawn together.

SUGAR: Not that I remember—but that can't be. How can two people spend so many years together and never see the sun come up?

CAMILLE: When I was a little girl, I always thought the rising sun would look like the golden sail of some big ship coming to carry me away, swelling bigger and bigger the nearer it got.

SUGAR: Well, you stay up here and keep a lookout for that boat with a golden sail—and anything else floats by. Something comes this way, you start shouting for help, y'understand? I'm going to see what I can find to cut myself out of here.

(*He disappears down the hole.*)

CAMILLE: It's just so dark and silent here tonight, it feels as if there's no one else alive. Like being marooned alone on some small island or—I don't know—the sole survivor of a sunken ship, drifting in a lifeboat all night long. Wouldn't that be awful, Sug? To be the sole survivor when your ship goes down. With no one else alive but you. Just you and all that water.

(*Silence.*)

It makes me nervous—waiting all alone up here for you.

(*Silence.*)

I'm talking to you, Sugar. Did you hear what I just said?

SUGAR (*unseen in the attic*): I heard it, every word, Camille. Don't worry, I won't be long in here. There must be something in the attic would do the job.

(*His arm and then head emerging through the hole.*)

And, look, you sure there's nothing we can eat up here? Hard candy, maybe? That would do me fine for now.

CAMILLE: You could stand to go a whole night without food for once, you know, and maybe lose a little of that weight. You didn't stuff yourself on silver bells and goldbricks all the time, this hole'd be big enough for you the way it is.

SUGAR: Yeah, well, it's not just me I'm worried about when it comes to starving.

CAMILLE: Who you think you foolin', Sug? I'm not the one keeps a stash of jelly beans beside the bed.

SUGAR: I wish I'd thought to bring them up the stairs with me tonight.

CAMILLE: It's no mystery how you come by your name, I'll tell you.

SUGAR: How many times Mama told you they called me Sugar 'cause everybody said I was the sweetest baby New Orleans ever saw?

(*Pause.*)

CAMILLE: Was there ever a baby born into a world like this? I don't recognize a thing about it.

SUGAR: Old world or new, I still need to eat.

CAMILLE: I promise you there's not a scrap of food in there. Not with all the roaches we would have. Go just find a saw or something you can use to get yourself out here. What if a boat comes by and you're still stuck in there?

SUGAR (*disappearing again*): All right, let me look and get this done.

(*Silence.*)

CAMILLE: You know, what you said before, I'm beginning to think you might be right. In this moonlight, everything looks so strange, so fresh. Maybe it's not the end of the world, this rising water.

SUGAR (*unseen in the attic*): I can't hear you. Somebody coming?

CAMILLE: No, no sign of anyone. (*Softer.*) I was just saying, though, maybe you were right before. It looks so different up here now. Maybe you and me, we could go back and start again.

(*Silence.*)

I mean, with everything disappearing—our house, our things—like you said, our past is being washed away. It's left us sort of standing on a mountaintop up here, like Noah's Ark coming to rest after all that rain.

(*Silence.*)

Oh, Sugar, you really think it's possible? You really think two people—the two of us—we could begin again?

SUGAR (*an arm and then his head emerging through the hole*): You calling me?

CAMILLE: What? No, I was just thinking out loud about what you said before.

SUGAR (*with only his arm and head visible*): What's that?

CAMILLE: About us going back to when we met and starting over fresh.

SUGAR: I was just teasing you, Camille, that's all. How's it possible, that, anyway, after all we've been through, you and me? How could we ever forget what we already know?

CAMILLE: But isn't that what people mean, they talk about forgive and forget? You let it go, all the anger, the hurt—

SUGAR: And then you spend the rest of your life pretending to forget.

CAMILLE: Isn't that what I had to do with you?

SUGAR: Camille, that was a long time ago.

CAMILLE: But never long enough. (*Sighs.*) I guess you right about forgetting. Neither one of us forgot it yet, what you done to me, even after all these years.

SUGAR: Well, it don't come up so much as it used to anymore.

CAMILLE: For you, it don't, maybe.

SUGAR (*slamming his hand on the roof*): Nothing I can ever do to make that right, is there?

(*Silence.*)

How many times you want an apology for one damn night? I've spent my whole life ever since saying I'm sorry for what I did to you that evening.

(*Silence.*)

You know, you're not the first woman to feel a belt across her back. And I haven't laid a hand on you in all this time. I haven't touched a bottle once. I've come home every night for thirty years. How many ways I got to prove to you I learned my lesson?

CAMILLE: Learning the lesson don't change needing that lesson in the first place.

SUGAR: Husbands have done far worse to wives and been forgiven.

CAMILLE: You still don't understand the way a single night can change everything between two people, do you?

SUGAR: You think that's something I don't know? The whole damn world can change from dusk to dawn. Go to bed thinking everything's OK, thinking you survived the worst; wake up with water filling up your house.

CAMILLE: But that's exactly what I'm saying, Sug. Tonight's a night that maybe everything could change between the two of us.

SUGAR: So you finally ready to forget what it was I done?

CAMILLE: Forget? No, you right about that. Nobody ever forgets nothing. Not really. But choosing what to remember, that's something we could do.

SUGAR: And what is it exactly you'd choose, Camille? What's the thing that you'd remember, you had your choice?

CAMILLE: Me? Yeah, our first Mardi Gras, I guess. A girl doesn't forget a night like that.

(*Pause.*)

And other things . . .

SUGAR: Like what?

CAMILLE: Like that other thing you always say I ought to put behind me.

SUGAR: If anything needs forgetting, it's that.

CAMILLE: You think a mother could ever forget something like that?

SUGAR: But how long can a person hang on to grief, Camille? The anger burns itself out, like a candle you cover with a glass. It flares, but then it eats up all the air inside and suffocates.

CAMILLE (*angrily*): When you hear me bring up anything about it last?

SUGAR: Just try to get that glass off the table then. It's a vacuum, stuck so tight it won't budge—but with something burned-out still inside.

CAMILLE: Yeah, maybe I was like that for awhile—stuck fast to what had happened. But you were just as bad the other way. Refusing to admit—

SUGAR: There wasn't nothing to admit. We didn't do anything wrong, Camille. Some things, there's nothing anyone can do to stop them happening.

(*Silence.*)

You don't think I would've rather died myself than anything happen to that little girl of ours. But you can't spend your whole damn life saying good-bye, Camille. Sooner or later, you got to stop looking over your shoulder. It'll turn you into a pillar of salt, just like Lot's wife, looking back all the time.

CAMILLE: Lot's wife must have been somebody's mama. That's what it means to have a child—spending the rest of your life always looking over your shoulder to be sure they're still trailing after you.

SUGAR: You live that way too long, Camille, after a while, it's like I say. All that's left of you is salt for rubbing into a wound that's always open.

CAMILLE: I'm not the one went searching for those pictures in the flood downstairs.

SUGAR: And I'm not saying I don't think of Suzie every day. But it's wrong to make of her this, I don't know, this little anchor still holds us fast to some awful morning thirty years ago.

(*Silence.*)

CAMILLE: It can't be done, can it? I mean, pretend the past is not some anchor keeping us in place.

SUGAR (*sighing*): Yeah, it's not that we can't go back and start again. It's that we can't help but go back, over and over again. You think your boat is getting somewhere, making headway, but really, you're chained to the bottom and just don't know it. We're sailing in a circle all the time.

CAMILLE: Oh, Sugar, what's ahead of us, you and me?

SUGAR: We went to bed tonight, I thought I knew.

CAMILLE: So did a lot of people already dead since then.

SUGAR: Well, we're not that.

CAMILLE: Not yet, at least.

(*Silence.*)

But tell you the truth—if that's what it is we're finally doing— I don't feel like I'm alive, either. In fact, I haven't felt like I'm alive in a long, long time now. Not like it felt when we first met.

SUGAR: You think it's any different for me?

(*Silence.*)

Probably the same for everyone. Just nobody ever dares put it into words.

CAMILLE: Suzie gone. Frankie lost. I don't know I feel I even deserve to be alive, you get right down to it.

SUGAR: How can we feel it's not all our fault, the things that happen?

(*Pause.*)

But maybe you right. Maybe this is some second chance for us tonight.

(*Silence.*)

(*Lights fade.*)

SCENE 2

(Lights rise. An hour later, now about 5:00 a.m. CAMILLE is lying on the roof. SUGAR is still in the hole.)

SUGAR: I never knew dying could be so boring.

CAMILLE: I thought you said we're gonna be OK up here.

SUGAR: Just a figure of speech, Camille. All I mean is, it's so damn boring stuck up here all night long.

CAMILLE: Well maybe if you'd thought to bring the radio up with you from downstairs, we'd have something to listen to right now.

SUGAR: The batteries were nearly dead already the time we went to bed. *(Pause.)* And anyway, they're not playing music on the radio tonight.

CAMILLE: No, they probably trying to figure out what in the hell's going on around here, just like us.

(Silence.)

SUGAR: I tell you, my back is killing me, stuck here in this hole. Let me change arms.

(He descends, and then the other arm emerges, followed by his head.)

CAMILLE: Be careful, Sug. You move too much, those jagged edges there will cut you to ribbons. Then what would we do, you bleeding to death on this rooftop without a boat in sight.

SUGAR (*struggling a bit in the hole*): Yeah, you right. I'm wedged in here too tight to climb up any higher. But damn my back is getting sore. I'd go lie down in the attic for a while, but I can feel the water around my feet. It's still inching up, I think.

CAMILLE: We got to entertain ourselves, that's what we got to do. Keep our minds off everything.

SUGAR: Entertain ourselves how?

CAMILLE: I don't know.

(*Pause.*)

We used to play a game when I was small. "Secrets," they called it.

SUGAR: Secrets?

CAMILLE: Yeah, you go back and forth, telling each other secrets you're not supposed to say.

SUGAR: What kind of secrets?

CAMILLE: Ones you don't want me to know about.

SUGAR: Then why would I tell you?

CAMILLE: Because we might as well be honest with each other if we're going to die tonight like you said before.

SUGAR: But what if we don't die? Then where would I be? You'd know my secret.

CAMILLE: What secret?

SUGAR: I mean if I had a secret.

CAMILLE: But you do have secrets.

SUGAR: What secrets?

CAMILLE: I don't know, like that time you walked in on Tina taking a bath.

SUGAR: You know about that?

CAMILLE: Of course I know about that. Tina was my best friend. She told me you really got an eyeful, too. She was afraid you were going to sit down on the edge of the tub and have a little chat with her.

SUGAR: I got flustered, that's all. It's not easy to back out of a room.

CAMILLE: Yeah, I bet it's hard when you can't even turn your eyes to find the doorknob.

SUGAR: It was an accident, walking in like that. How was I to know she was in there?

CAMILLE: And she told me about that other time you saw her naked.

SUGAR: I don't remember that.

CAMILLE: How could you forget? It was that weekend we went down to Orange Beach and shared the cabin with her and Buddy. Come on, Sugar. This is our chance to reveal—after all these years together—to really reveal what's been going on inside us, who we really are.

SUGAR: I don't think that's such a good idea.

CAMILLE: Well, if you're too chicken, then I'll have to start.

SUGAR: It's really not a good idea.

CAMILLE: When we used to, you know what I mean, in bed, I'd pretend you were Sean Connery.

SUGAR: The actor?

CAMILLE: Of course the actor.

SUGAR: But he was so much older than you.

CAMILLE: Yeah, I liked that.

SUGAR: Why did you have to pretend at all? I was strong, handsome.

CAMILLE: Handsome? No, I wouldn't say handsome. Solid, maybe.

SUGAR: Solid? You mean chunky?

CAMILLE: Well, not solid. Not exactly. But, you know, rugged. How's that? You were rugged.

SUGAR: Rugged? Yeah, that would be OK.

CAMILLE: And so was Sean.

SUGAR: Sean? You called him by his first name?

CAMILLE: Well, what do you think I was pretending? "Oh, Mr. Connery, you're divine, you're wonderful." Of course I called him "Sean."

SUGAR: And what did he call you?

CAMILLE: I don't know. You were playing him. What did you call me?

SUGAR: I wasn't playing anybody. I was playing myself. I mean, I was just myself.

CAMILLE: But you must have been pretending I was somebody else.

SUGAR: No, I wasn't.

CAMILLE: Liar.

SUGAR: Oh sure, the night I walked in on Tina in the bathtub, maybe she crossed my mind.

CAMILLE: You slept with Tina!

SUGAR: No, of course not. But it was only natural, seeing her, you know, leaning back in the tub with her eyes closed. How could I not think of her that night?

CAMILLE: Just the one night?

SUGAR: Well, maybe a couple times after that. I don't know, it was all so long ago.

CAMILLE: So when was the last time you were thinking about my best friend like that?

SUGAR: I don't remember the last time—

CAMILLE: You thought about her every time, didn't you?

SUGAR: No, not every time. (*Pause.*) Sometimes I'd think of Madonna.

CAMILLE: The singer? The one who wears those funnels on her breasts.

SUGAR: They're not funnels. It's a costume.

CAMILLE: So I'm lying there thinking you're whispering, "Oh, my darling, my darling," and you're really sighing, "Oh, Madonna, Madonna."

SUGAR: No, of course not. That sounds stupid. "Oh, Madonna, Madonna." I call her "Louise."

CAMILLE: Louise? Why Louise?

SUGAR: That's her real name. Madonna Louise Veronica Ciccone.

CAMILLE: I can't believe you've been unfaithful to me with a girl who wears funnels on her tits.

SUGAR: They're not funnels. They're just part of her costume. And anyway, it's your own fault if I had an affair with a beautiful rock star.

CAMILLE: My fault? You cheat on me with a girl with tin tits and somehow I'm the guilty party.

SUGAR: Once you stopped singing to me in bed, I had to find someone else to take your place.

CAMILLE: I never sang to you in bed.

SUGAR: Sure you did. Remember? You used to lie in the dark afterwards, when everything was so still, and you'd sing those funny little songs to me.

CAMILLE: What songs?

SUGAR: You know. (*Singing.*) "*If ever I cease to love.*"

CAMILLE: Oh, you're out of your mind. It must have been Madonna that used to sing to you.

SUGAR: Come on, and sing it with me.

CAMILLE: No, I won't sing it with you. It was some other girl used to sing to you in bed.

SUGAR: You know there's never been another girl in my bed. Just you.

CAMILLE: And Tina. And—what do you call her?—Louise.

SUGAR: Come on. Sing to me.

CAMILLE: I don't even know how it goes, your stupid song.

SUGAR: Sure you do. (*Singing.*) "*If ever I cease to love.*"

CAMILLE (*without enthusiasm*): "*If ever I cease to love.*"

SUGAR: Remember? (*Singing.*) "*The moon would turn to green cream cheese, if ever I cease to love.*" (*Speaking.*) Now sing the whole thing to me, the way you used to.

CAMILLE: This is stupid. I'm not singing it.

SUGAR: But you do remember singing to me in bed, right?

CAMILLE: No.

SUGAR: Don't be angry with me. I told you this was a dangerous game, telling secrets. (*Pause.*) So you got any other secrets you been keeping from me?

CAMILLE: None you ever gonna find out about.

SUGAR: Now that's enough to make a husband worry the rest of his life, something like that coming out of his wife's mouth.

(*Silence.*)

CAMILLE: All you need to worry about is how much I love you. And I love you plenty. You know that.

(*Silence.*)

SUGAR: Be honest with you, I can't say I know why you love me at all.

(*Pause.*)

CAMILLE: I'll tell you then.

(*Pause.*)

Just after Frankie left the last time, stormed out of the house for good after the fight the two of you'd had that night, I saw you standing in the hallway, closing the door to his bedroom. You pulled it shut so gently, you broke my heart. And I couldn't shake the sight of you, standing there before his door, like someone lost, not knowing where to go.

(*Silence.*)

SUGAR: I have to pull the door shut every night on Frankie's room to have a chance of getting any sleep at all. I can't bear to see them in the dark, his things. The model planes still on his desk, the posters curling on the walls.

(*Pause.*)

I can't sleep I know his door is open.

(*Silence.*)

CAMILLE: I think love's got a whole lot more to do with pity than people are willing to admit.
SUGAR: Pity? That's what you think love is?

CAMILLE: How many times you've taken pity on me, Sug?

SUGAR: When I ever show you any pity?

CAMILLE: How many times just tonight you pitied me how scared I was? How many times you pitied me getting old and lied how pretty I still look? How many times you pitied our boy, out there somewhere doing what he does? The heart don't break for someone it don't love.

SUGAR: Well, I know I give *you* plenty to pity. I guess that's what makes me so lovable, huh?

CAMILLE: I'm not joking, Sugar. You said you'd rather've died than it was Suzie we found that morning. You think that's not taking pity, you'd rather die than someone else? And the longer two people been together, the more you feel it, don't you, that sympathy for what the other person's going through?

SUGAR: I don't know I'd call all that pity.

CAMILLE: I don't mean you feel better than the other person—you know, superior, something like that. Just your heart breaks for them, don't it, somebody you love? That's what I'm talking about, I guess. That kind of pity.

SUGAR: So it was nothing but pity, then, you taking Sean Connery into your bed?

CAMILLE: Yeah, just like it couldn't 've been anything but pity, Madonna letting you sleep with her.

SUGAR: You know, woman, you some bad.

CAMILLE: Lucky for you.

SUGAR: And lucky for Sean Connery.

(*Silence.*)

The stars are out tonight.

CAMILLE: I know. It's so dark with all the power off, you can see them, every one. When you think the last time was anyone could see so many stars over New Orleans?

SUGAR: Go back a hundred years, at least.

CAMILLE: Oh, more than that. Two hundred, maybe more.

SUGAR: All those stars, and so much water.

CAMILLE: All the way to the horizon.

SUGAR: Reminds me of where my father and I used to fish—when I was a boy, I mean—down in the marsh. That's where he told me that ghost story of his.

CAMILLE: I can't believe he'd tell a little child a story like that. Hot as it is up here, just thinking of that mother and her baby makes me shiver.

SUGAR: Well, it gave me more than goose bumps, hearing it the way Daddy told it.

CAMILLE: It wasn't like the way you said to me?

SUGAR: To be the same, I'd have to whisper it so close to your face you could smell my breath—but in darkness so black you couldn't even see my lips.

CAMILLE: How's that possible?

SUGAR: We were deep in the marsh, way back down one of those winding canals off the ship channel, fishing speckled trout. It was already nearly three, so my father tried to start the engine. He pulled on the cord till I thought he would rip the top off the motor, but it didn't even cough.

CAMILLE: How old were you?

SUGAR: I don't know. Nine. Maybe ten.

CAMILLE: You were just a baby.

SUGAR: No, I wasn't a baby. I was ten years old.

CAMILLE: Oh, you were a baby. Ten years old.

SUGAR: OK, then, I was a baby. Anyway, bobbing there in our little boat, Daddy changed the spark plugs, cleaned the lines, went through the whole drill. But when he popped the cover back on and tugged the cord again—nothing. We were stuck. And hunkered back in the marsh the way we were, we hadn't seen another boat in a couple of hours.

CAMILLE: So what did your father do?

SUGAR: What he always did. He pulled a bottle out of the ice chest.

CAMILLE: But what about you? You must have been frightened, a little child like you.

SUGAR: There used to be a saying when I was a boy: "Nobody but God can whup my daddy, and God better watch his step." As long as Daddy was leaning back against the bow drinking Dixies, it was just another fishing trip as far as I was concerned. I knew Mama would be upset, our being late and all—and I was worried about that because I knew what would happen if she made too much of a fuss when we got home. But afraid of being stranded out in the marsh? I didn't have the slightest idea how much trouble we were in.

CAMILLE: So what did you do?

SUGAR: My father and I sat there till dusk. Every once in a while, Daddy would stand up on the bench and look for another boat, but nobody else was still out, and we were too far off the channel to catch a tow with the shrimp boats coming in from the Gulf. He was still in a pretty good mood, though. After he'd take a look, he would say, "I'd better send up a flare." And he'd unzip his pants and take a piss, standing on the seat. I guess it was all the beer he'd been drinking.

CAMILLE: And what about you?

SUGAR: Me? I'd had a little too much sun by then. Hot as it was, I started getting chills. Fever, I suppose.

CAMILLE: Keep a child out there on the water all day till he gets sick?

SUGAR: I was sick all right, but we had a bigger problem to deal with. I could already hear them lifting out of the grass before I could see them. At first, I thought it was an engine. But there weren't any boats when I looked, just small dark clouds hovering, twitching over the mudflats. I didn't know what they were—smoke, fog? But as the roaring got louder, I looked down at my hands. They were seething with mosquitoes.

CAMILLE: Mosquitoes?

SUGAR: It was weird; I hadn't felt a thing. Maybe it was the fever, I don't know, but I watched these bugs crawling all over themselves like it was somebody else's hands they were biting. And then, calm as could be, I plunged both arms into the water. With my face close to the canal, the racket from all those little wings overhead was unbelievable.

CAMILLE: And what was your father doing all this time?

SUGAR: Daddy had fallen asleep in the bow. So I crawled beside him, and when I got close enough to see him in the dark, his face and neck were so thick with mosquitoes he looked like he'd grown a black beard. I tried to call out to wake him, but my mouth was full of them before I could even say his name. I choked on mosquitoes, spitting them out into the water. My coughing woke him up. By then, they were in our eyes. I think my eyelids were starting to swell shut from all the bites. Next thing I know, Daddy throws me overboard and jumps in beside me.

CAMILLE: My God. I can't believe you never told me this before.

SUGAR: He's spitting the bugs out even while he's shouting at me. He gets his shirt off and throws it over our heads like a little tent. Then he pulls us underwater—to kill the mosquitoes still trapped under the shirt. "Vicious little bastards, ain't they?" he shouts at me even though he's just inches away when we come up again. Daddy says the edges of the shirt have to stay in the water. But it's so dark you can't tell where the water begins.

CAMILLE: That's horrifying.

SUGAR: It's the strangest feeling, floating there in this absolutely pitch-black darkness. Every now and then, I start to panic. Then he talks to me, calms me down. I get used to it after a while, I guess, because I'm falling asleep when something brushes my leg and makes me jump. I ask Daddy, "Did you just feel anything?" But before he can answer, something hits us both at the same time, coming between us, I think.

CAMILLE: An alligator?

SUGAR: Alligator? No, a shark, most likely. That afternoon, I'd seen one easing through the water, maybe fifty feet out, sliding back and forth as easy as you please. It wasn't all that big a shark— five, six foot—but big enough, I knew. So there I am, floating in the dark, remembering what I'd seen that afternoon. Not to mention Daddy, he's not under the shirt with me anymore. I call out for him and start paddling forward, trying to find him. But then I hear his voice shouting to stay still. That's when I feel it again, its side scraping my leg like sandpaper. I'm crying, with Daddy half whispering, "Hush, hush, they'll hear you." That really scares me. It hasn't occurred to me there might be more than one shark. "And don't take a crap," he warns. "They love the smell of shit."

CAMILLE: So what happens?

(*Pause.*)

SUGAR: Nothing. We don't move for a minute or two—in the dark inside that shirt, all by myself, it felt like hours—and that was it. Gone. Daddy reaches out and grabs me and gets us organized again under the shirt. Only this time I'm hanging on to his neck so tight he says I'm gonna choke him. (*Pause.*) So that's when he tells me the story.

CAMILLE: You were just ten years old?

SUGAR: Worse things happen to kids. It did make me sad, though, the story. I didn't know who I felt worse for, the captain or his little girl. But that's how we got through the night. That and the singing.

CAMILLE: Singing?

SUGAR: After all those hours in the water, my father's having a hard time staying awake, I think, because all of a sudden he starts singing. In his whole life, it was the only song I ever heard him sing. (*Pause.*) Let me see I remember it. (*Singing.*)

> *If the ocean were whiskey,*
> *And I were a duck,*
> *I'd swim to the bottom*
> *And never come up.*

But the ocean's not whiskey,
And I'm not a duck,
So I'll play the jack of diamonds
And trust to my luck.

He just keeps singing those same verses over and over again, like a chant more than a song, really. Then I start singing.

(*Pause.*)

It must have sounded strange out there in that dark marsh, those two voices carrying across the water. We kept at it a long time, waiting for the light.

CAMILLE: The whole night in the water?

SUGAR: The whole damn night. Then, when the sun finally rises, we haul ourselves up into the boat and try the motor again. There's nothing doing, though, so Daddy ties a line to a bow cleat and, with water up to his chest, drags the boat along the shelf of the mudflats for hours, it seems, until he's hauled us to the mouth of the canal. Out in the channel, we see a shrimper heading in after a night of trawling. We get up on the benches and swing the life vests over our heads, shouting like crazy people, "Hey, over here, over here."

(*Silence.*)

I've never known another feeling like when that shrimp boat, still a hundred, two hundred yards out, swung its bow toward us. You'll see when the rescue boats show up here. There's nothing else like it—seeing a boat coming to save you after you've survived a night on the water.

CAMILLE: My God, what a night.

SUGAR: So that's how I heard my father's story about the captain who buried his wife and daughter at sea.

CAMILLE: He say anything else about it, his story?

SUGAR: Yeah, one other thing. Years later, just before he died.

CAMILLE: What's that?

SUGAR: He said they all end the same way, sea stories—in madness or in death.

CAMILLE: And what about this story?

SUGAR: It's not a story. It's true.

CAMILLE: But how does it end?

SUGAR: End? With the singing, I guess, with the two of us singing, singing about whiskey and cards and a drunken duck—adrift in that black water, in that dark marsh, the mosquitoes hovering over our heads like death, and the two of us singing, singing until the sun comes up.

(*An alarm goes off in the distance.*)

CAMILLE: What's that, Sugar? Is someone coming? A rescue boat?

SUGAR: I don't see anyone. Not from down here. You see anything?

CAMILLE (*looking in all directions*): No, nothing.

SUGAR: Might be, it's just a house alarm going off in somebody's attic.

CAMILLE: Why now?

SUGAR: They'll all start wailing, one after another, as the batteries go down. It's meant to be a warning the system's dying.

(*More alarms go off in the distance.*)

CAMILLE: It sounds like moaning when it's far away.

SUGAR: And like screams up close.

CAMILLE: I can't stand the sound of it.

SUGAR: They say it's full of fire, not water, but that's what I'd guess it sounds like down in hell.

CAMILLE: They must be on their way by now.

SUGAR: Who?

CAMILLE: The boats. They'll be here soon, won't they, Sug? Help's got to be on its way by now. The sun's nearly up.

SUGAR: Those boats, they'd better be here soon. A couple hours, that rising sun will turn the attic hotter than an oven and make this roof one sizzlin' skillet, we're still trapped up here.

CAMILLE: You wait and see. The sun comes up, the sky will fill with helicopters, and the water's gonna be so thick with rescue boats, we'll be able to walk to high ground we want to.

SUGAR: It's nearly dawn and no sign yet of anybody.

CAMILLE: The only thing you need to worry about is what you want for breakfast once they save us.

(*Pause.*)

SUGAR: At least we'll finally get to watch the sun come up together, you and me.

(*Silence.*)

CAMILLE: Let's sing, Sugar. Like you and your daddy did. Let's just keep singing till the sun comes up and those boats get here.

SUGAR: Sing what?

CAMILLE (*singing*):

> *If ever I cease to love,*
> *If ever I cease to love,*
> *The moon would turn to green cream cheese,*
> *If ever I cease to love.*

SUGAR (*laughing, then singing*):

> *If ever I cease to love,*
> *If ever I cease to love,*
> *May cows lay eggs and fish grow legs,*
> *If ever I cease to love.*

(*CAMILLE joins in with him. More alarms go off and begin to drown them out as they continue to sing to each other.*)

If ever I cease to love,
If ever I cease to love,
We'll all turn into cats and dogs,
If ever I cease to love.

(*They stop singing and look at each other. Wailing alarms grow louder and more numerous and light slowly brightens to full noon as they wait for help that does not come. They turn to face the audience. The alarms reach a crescendo. Blackout.*)

SHOTGUN

×✗×

Shotgun was first produced in a National New Play Network Rolling World Premiere at Southern Rep Theatre (2009), Orlando Shakespeare Theater (2010), and Florida Studio Theatre (2010). The National New Play Network Rolling World Premiere of *Shotgun* began at Southern Rep Theatre, Aimée Hayes, Producing Artistic Director, in New Orleans on May 9, 2009. It was directed by Valerie Curtis-Newton with the following cast:

BEAU	Rus Blackwell
EUGENE	Alex Lemonier
DEX	Lance E. Nichols
MATTIE	Donna Duplantier
WILLIE	Kenneth Brown, Jr.

Scenic design by Geoffrey Hall
Lighting design by Patti West
Costumes by Kelly James-Penot
Original compositions/sound design by Eric Shimelonis
Production Stage Manager: Sarah Zoghbi

CHARACTERS
(in order of appearance)

BEAU HARLAN, white carpenter in his mid-thirties
EUGENE HARLAN, Beau's sixteen-year-old son
DEXTER (DEX) GODCHAUX, Mattie's father, in his early sixties
MATTIE GODCHAUX, black woman in her thirties
CLARENCE (WILLIE) WILLIAMS, Mattie's black ex-boyfriend,
about her age

PLACE
New Orleans.

TIME
December 2005.

Note: A New Orleans "shotgun double" is a duplex with the two sides of the house laid out as mirror images; one has to pass through a room to get to the next room (there is no hallway except beside the bathroom). The front porch, often as wide as the house, is shared; the front steps may be shared as well. The set design should allow unimpeded movement back and forth between the porch and the kitchen as the scenes shift.

ACT I

SCENE 1

(*Late afternoon. Front porch of a New Orleans shotgun duplex with a "For Rent" sign on one of the two front doors. Christmas decorations are up on the occupied side. BEAU and EUGENE enter. With the rental section of the newspaper in hand, BEAU climbs the stairs, knocks at the door without the sign, then returns to the bottom of the steps. DEX opens the front door but doesn't step onto the porch.*)

DEX: Help you?

BEAU: Yes, sir. Other side of your shotgun still for rent?

DEX: Lose your house in the flood?

BEAU (*nodding*): Over in Gentilly, off Elysian Fields.

DEX: Y'all get much water there?

BEAU: Wound up in the attic before it was done.

DEX: Sorry to hear that.

BEAU: Lot of people in the same boat, I guess.

DEX (*stepping onto the porch*): Yeah, you looking at one of 'em.

BEAU: Thought y'all didn't get any water over here in Algiers, this side of the river.

DEX: Didn't. This my daughter's house. Nothing but a little wind damage all she got. Branch come down on her shed out back. Couple tiles off the roof. Probably all I would've had, too, the levees don't give way like they done.

BEAU: Where you from, then?

DEX: The Lower Ninth.

BEAU: They say it was real bad down there, huh?

DEX: Bad? (*He laughs.*) Tell you what, mister, "bad" don't come close to covering what went on that day. One minute you standing on your porch just like this; next minute you getting washed up onto somebody's roof like you been shipwrecked on a desert island in the middle of the ocean.

BEAU: Sounds like you lucky to be alive.

DEX: I hadn't come out on the porch when I did, wouldn't be here to tell the tale. (*Pause.*) Don't let nobody ever tell you the world's gonna end in fire. I done seen how the world ends. (*Pause.*) Lost a lot of my people that day.

EUGENE: You not the only one lost somebody.

BEAU (*eyeing his son into silence*): Where we lived, the storm was long gone before we saw any water at all.

EUGENE: Yeah, and ten minutes later, we're up in the attic, and the flood's still rising.

DEX: My whole life I lived down there. In that same house since I got married. And before that 'round the corner at my mama's house.

BEAU: Well, I guess you lucky to have a daughter, at least, on high ground. And a little high ground's just what we looking for, me and my boy.

DEX: Look, mister, the other half of my daughter's shotgun, I'm gonna take it myself.

EUGENE: Then how come the "For Rent" sign's still up?

BEAU: Eugene.

DEX: Didn't think to take it down yet, son, that's all. We only just decided last night.

(*DEX takes down the sign.*)

BEAU: Well, sorry to hear it's not available. We been staying in a motel up in LaPlace since October. Kind of crowded, though, with just the one room. We keep getting on each other's nerves, the boy and me, living on top of each other.

DEX (*sitting down in a porch chair*): Yeah, know what you talking about. Me and Mattie, well, the girl's got her own way of doing things.

BEAU: Not much else to choose from, though. People got apartments didn't flood, they've doubled, tripled the rent. Nothing like what I can manage on a carpenter's pay.

DEX: Why don't y'all go get yourselves one of them FEMA trailers? Park it in your driveway.

BEAU: Signed up for it soon as we heard about them. FEMA says maybe by summer they'll have one for us.

DEX: Summer?

BEAU: Some kind of bottleneck, they say. And now they even giving us trouble about paying our motel bill. They want to see last year's pay stubs, insurance policies, income tax—I don't know what all. And most of the papers they talking about, it all got washed away in the flood.

DEX: Sons of bitches, every damn one of them FEMA bastards.

BEAU: I don't know where they think we gonna live, they cut us off like they want to do. Those motel people, they talking better than two thousand dollars a month for one damn room. That's why we thought maybe this place, it would do us till we figured out what we gonna do next.

(*MATTIE, in business attire, enters.*)

DEX: Here comes my daughter now. Sorry we couldn't help y'all.

MATTIE: Help with what?

BEAU: How you do, ma'am? Your father was just explaining the other half of your shotgun's not for rent anymore.

MATTIE: What do you mean, Daddy, it's not for rent anymore?

DEX: Yeah, you know what we talked about last night—me moving in your other side.

MATTIE: I never said yes to that. (*Turning to BEAU and EUGENE.*) Could you excuse us for just a minute, please?

BEAU: Yes, ma'am. C'mon, Gene.

(*They withdraw and seem to argue.*)

MATTIE: I told you last night, I can't pay my mortgage without the rent from next door.

DEX: They open up the shop again, I'll pay you all the rent you want.

MATTIE: I'm the one drove you over there the day you went to see. Nothing's left—the lathes, the presses, the drills so thick with rust it looks like scabs all over them. And everything else looted or smashed. Now how's Mr. Mullins gonna reopen with his business in ruins?

DEX: There's not another machinist in this city can touch the work I do.

MATTIE: I know, Daddy. Everybody said you were the best machinist in the shop. Truth be told, you ran the place. But there's just no job for you to go back to.

(*Pause.*)

DEX: Anyway, what you doing thinking about renting to whites? They got their own neighborhoods.

MATTIE: Not anymore they don't.

DEX: Plenty of black folks just as much in need of a place. Think they got whites in this city gonna rent to them? Girl, you got an obligation to take care of your own people first.

MATTIE: Daddy, I know it's hard losing your house—and your job on top of that. And I know this goes against your grain. But I got to rent the place to somebody with money—and soon. I've lost four months' rent already.

DEX: You asking for trouble, you do this, Mattie. Trust an old man. Mixing black and white, it's nothing but a jug of gasoline looking for a match.

MATTIE: Mister?

(*BEAU and EUGENE approach.*)

Seems as if there's been a little misunderstanding here. Turns out the place is still available. Six hundred a month, and I pay the water.

BEAU: Six hundred? That's the best deal we come across since we started looking.

MATTIE: Same as before the flood. I'm not one to take advantage of other people's bad luck.

BEAU: Well, you just about the only one who isn't. And six hundred's a whole lot better than what that motel costs we staying in.

MATTIE: You take it, I'll need a month's deposit plus the first month's rent up front.

BEAU: If you can wait till I get paid the end of the week, I can let you have it then. (*He takes out his wallet.*) A hundred fifty dollars hold the place till Saturday?

MATTIE: That'll do. But maybe you ought to take a look, see whether it's what you want before you put down any money.

BEAU: Anything gets us out of that motel we living in's gonna suit us just fine.

MATTIE: All the same, it's got just the one bedroom. Like my side.

BEAU: One of us can sleep in the front room.

MATTIE: Yeah, that's what my father's doing, too.

DEX: A broken-down old sofa stuffed with gravel, that's where my daughter has me sleeping. You ever hear of such a thing, a child treating her own father that a way?

MATTIE: The sofa's not five years old, Daddy. There's nothing wrong with it.

DEX: How would you know? You don't sleep on it.

MATTIE (*to BEAU*): I don't know how many times I've offered to switch with him, let him have the bedroom.

DEX: You think I'd let my little girl sleep on a sofa feels like the one you got? How could I rest at night knowing you was up front tossing and turning on them sacks of stones you call cushions?

BEAU: To have my own place again, I'd be glad for even a sofa to sleep on.

MATTIE: Don't mind him. He loves to complain. (*To DEX.*) I don't know what you and Mama would've talked about all your lives, you didn't spend the whole day whining about something or other.

DEX: You leave your mother out of this, God rest her. At least she fixed me decent food to eat.

MATTIE: You're supposed to be on a diet. You know what the doctor said. (*Pause.*) Can we talk about this later, Daddy? (*Pause.*) You'll have to forgive my father. So . . . I'll need references.

BEAU: I haven't rented from anybody in ten, twelve years. Ever since we bought our own place.

MATTIE: You lose it in the flood?

BEAU: I was telling your father, yeah. But the contractor I'm working for, he can vouch for me. I'll give you his number. (*Pause.*) Wouldn't be furnished, would it?

MATTIE: Well, the last tenants didn't come back after the storm. I kept holding it for them, but they finally decided they better stay put in Houston. Still haven't come for their furniture, though.

DEX: You ought to sell all that stuff, cover the rent you lost waiting for them to make up their mind.

MATTIE (*ignoring her father*): You two can use their things—at least until they come get it all.

BEAU: We weren't able to salvage much from the house. What the flood didn't ruin, the mold got afterwards.

MATTIE: Daddy, go get the key.

(*Unhappy, DEX goes into the house.*)

BEAU: By the way, ma'am, name's Beau Harlan. And this is my boy, Eugene.

MATTIE: Pleased to meet the both of you. I'm Mattie Godchaux. And my father's Dexter—but don't ever call him that. Hates his name. He goes by "Dex."

DEX (*returning*): Can't find the key.

MATTIE: Can't find it? It's hanging on the back of the kitchen door where it always is.

DEX: Must be lost. Go look for yourself.

MATTIE (*entering the house*): It better not be hanging on the back of that door when I get there.

DEX: It ain't on its hook, I told you. (*MATTIE exits.*) You sure you want this place, mister? You know the neighborhood, it's all black.

EUGENE: I told you, Daddy. We're gonna be the only white people over here.

DEX: Boy's right. You sure you wouldn't be more comfortable somewhere else? Uptown, maybe? And you wouldn't have to cross the bridge every day, you lived over there. Ought to think about all the tolls you'd save living on the other side of the river. It adds up, I'll tell you.

BEAU: We're way past worrying where we'd be more comfortable, Mr. Godchaux.

DEX: I mean, it don't bother me none, you living next door. But some people, you know how they are. And everybody seems to be on edge right now.

BEAU: Can't blame them, with what we all been through.

DEX: Just hate to see you or the boy wind up with any more trouble on your plate than you already got.

BEAU: It's not trouble we're looking for, Mr. Godchaux. A place to live's all we're after.

MATTIE (*returning*): I can't understand it. That key's always on the back of the door. (*Pause.*) You sure you didn't stick it somewhere and forget about it?

DEX (*checking his pockets*): Well, how you like that? Here's the little sucker. Forgot I shoved it in there.

MATTIE (*smirking as she snatches the key from DEX*): So let me show you your place.

(*MATTIE unlocks the other front door. BEAU and EUGENE start to climb the front steps. Lights fade.*)

SCENE 2

(The kitchen in BEAU's side of the shotgun the following Saturday night, which happens to be New Year's Eve. EUGENE is searching for plates and silverware in cabinets. BEAU is ready to serve the unappetizing dinner he has made—some kind of stew or casserole. They eat throughout the scene.)

EUGENE: Well, I hope you're happy. You got us eating off other people's plates in somebody else's house on the wrong side of the river.

BEAU: You'd rather still be sharing that motel room on Airline Highway?

EUGENE: I'd rather be back in our own house again.

BEAU: Think I wouldn't, too? Think I don't wish none of this had ever happened?

EUGENE: But we just forget it all and move on—that your plan?

BEAU: Plan? All I know to do is keep swimming until you see dry ground.

EUGENE: What's this, then? Some little island we swum up to?

BEAU: We got to have a place to stay.

EUGENE: So let's move back into our own house. It's not so bad.

BEAU: Not so bad? You helped me gut the place. What do we got left? Nothing but walls of studs covered in black mold and a roof with a hole knocked through it.

EUGENE: You supposed to be a carpenter. We can fix the house ourselves.

BEAU: With no electricity and no gas? That's where we supposed
to live?

EUGENE: Other people doing it.

BEAU: Living by candlelight in the cold without any heat? Eating
out of an ice chest? You'd rather that to this?

EUGENE: Better than living over this side of the river surrounded
by strangers.

BEAU: This neighborhood's just about the only one we can afford
right now. And once school starts after the holidays, you'll
make some friends.

EUGENE: Friends? This school over here, Daddy, it's all black.
Those new friends of mine gonna beat the crap out of me.

BEAU: A big football player like you? And they gonna be thrilled to
death to have you on their team.

EUGENE: It's 5A, the school. They went to the state playoffs three
years running.

BEAU: You'll do fine.

EUGENE: You got any idea how big they are, the players on a 5A
team? How fast?

BEAU: The coaches will treat you fair.

EUGENE: Fair won't be enough, not with what I'm up against over
here. (*Pause.*) I was gonna start this year, there'd been a season.
Coach Farris already told me last summer I was gonna start.

BEAU: Well, maybe by next fall, your old school'll be open again.

EUGENE: Who you kidding? Worse than our house, that place.
Everything's still sitting there rotting—books, curtains,
carpets—

BEAU: They got to be planning on doing something with it. They
can't just wait around until the school falls down on itself.

EUGENE: Even if they fix it up, who's gonna come back, anyway?
Everybody I went to school with, they living in Houston now
or Atlanta or who the hell knows where. Next fall's senior year,
my last chance to make first string.

BEAU: Look, Gene, I know it's been hard on you, all this. I'm not
suggesting otherwise.

EUGENE: Yeah, well, you're not the one has to go to a new school with a bunch of black bastards gonna kick my ass every day.

BEAU: You don't use language like that in my house, boy.

EUGENE: This ain't your house, Daddy. Don't you remember? You living in Miss Godchaux's house now. You nothing but a . . . a tenant, that's all you are.

BEAU: It won't be like before the flood, babe. Things have changed. These people you'll be going to school with, they been through the same as us.

EUGENE: Same as us? They lose their house, their school? They haven't lost a thing, these people over this side of the river.

BEAU: Everybody down here lost something. Even if it was nothing else but watching New Orleans die.

EUGENE: I seen more than just a city die.

BEAU: Yeah, I know you did. But what we gonna do, Gene, we don't keep swimming? Give up and drown? That's what you want to do?

EUGENE: What I want to do is go back home. Heat or no heat. Lights or no lights. Go live there and fix the place.

BEAU: And how am I supposed to pay for that? The insurance company switched adjustors on us. Now they say we got to start our claim all over again.

EUGENE: We move back home, all this rent money could go to fix the house instead.

BEAU: You don't know what building supplies cost right now, boy. And there's so much demand, they won't sell you more than nine panels of sheetrock at a time.

EUGENE: We don't rent, that's six hundred dollars extra every month we got to spend.

BEAU: That don't even get us started, Gene.

EUGENE: Then apply for a loan or something.

BEAU: Who's going to lend us money? We got no collateral except a ruined house and that old rattletrap of a pickup truck out front.

EUGENE: I told you not to buy that piece of junk.

BEAU: Well, what was I gonna do, stuck in Baton Rouge after the flood without a car? I can't get myself to jobs, I can't get work. And I don't work, you and me, we're still sleeping on cots on that basketball court in that shelter. You prefer that to this? (*Pause.*) No, I didn't think so.

EUGENE: So apply to the government.

BEAU: I would apply, there was anything to apply for. The government stop telling us, this, it's all our own fault for living down here, and they get around to actually doing something, I'd be first in line to apply.

EUGENE: So what are you saying?

BEAU: I'm saying we need a place to stay until we got some money coming in.

EUGENE: So we're stuck here forever?

(*The conversation is interrupted by a knock at the front door.*)

BEAU: Let me see who this could be.

(*BEAU goes to the offstage front door while EUGENE sulkily picks at his food. BEAU returns with MATTIE, holding half of a pie. She's overheard their quarreling through the wall and wants to assure herself she hasn't made a mistake renting to them.*)

MATTIE: Just wanted to wish you a happy New Year's Eve and make sure you were settling in all right.

BEAU: Yes, ma'am, just fine. It's real comfortable.

MATTIE: I brought you over half a buttermilk pie I baked today.

BEAU: You needn't have gone to the trouble.

MATTIE: My father already ate the other half. And I leave it in my kitchen, he'll finish off the whole thing by morning.

EUGENE: I never heard of buttermilk pie before. Sounds awful, you ask me.

MATTIE: It's sweeter than it sounds. (*Pause.*) Like some people, I guess.

BEAU (*before EUGENE can respond*): It'll be real nice having a home-cooked dessert.

MATTIE: I suppose you haven't had much home-cooked anything since the flood.

BEAU: No, this is the first meal for us in a long time didn't feature bologna sandwiches and potato chips. (*Pause.*) You care to join us for dinner? I made plenty.

MATTIE (*looking at BEAU's unappetizing food*): That's kind of you, but I've got a meatloaf in the oven. (*Pause.*) I imagine you've had a difficult time of it these last few months.

BEAU: Like everybody else, I guess.

MATTIE: That doesn't mean you don't deserve a piece of pie on Saturday night. (*Pause.*) Well, I better be going and get out your way.

BEAU: Appreciate it, ma'am, we really do. Let me see you out.

(*BEAU and MATTIE exit. EUGENE tastes the pie, likes it, and eats more. Lights fade.*)

(The front porch of the shotgun. Late afternoon. MATTIE is taking down Christmas decorations. BEAU returns home after a day of work, a carpenter's tool belt over his shoulder.)

BEAU: I was starting to think you planned on leaving those up till Mardi Gras.

MATTIE: My father kept promising to take them down. I finally figured out I don't do it myself, I'll have these lights up all year round. (*Pause.*) So how things going?

BEAU: I'm working on a house over in Lakeview. People say they gonna move back in soon as we done. They'll be the only ones on the block, they do.

(MATTIE has trouble taking down the decorations.)

Here, let me give you a hand.

(BEAU helps her.)

MATTIE: But paying a mortgage every month on a house you can't live in—and then rent for somewhere else on top of that. They got to do something, those people.

BEAU: Everywhere you turn, over there, nothing but houses cut in half by the water, others sitting in the middle of the street on top of cars.

MATTIE: I haven't been to see. Afraid I'd wind up with a flat tire.

BEAU: It's like somebody went up and down the street with a sack of ten-penny nails and a hole in the bottom of it.

MATTIE: Just try and get it fixed, you pick up a nail. A man at work told us he went to three different service stations before he found one willing to fix a flat. Not enough help, they say. And the one said yes, he had to leave the tire till the next day.

BEAU: The way things are, forget what's coming at you down the end of the road. In this city, you don't keep your eyes right in front of you all the time, watching where your next step's gonna land, you'll find yourself knee-deep in serious trouble before you can turn around.

(*WILLIE enters.*)

MATTIE: Speaking of trouble.

WILLIE: Hey, girl.

MATTIE: Clarence, I haven't been a girl in twenty years.

WILLIE: In my eyes, baby, you just the way you looked in high school.

MATTIE: Yeah, and you ain't changed in all that time, neither. Still don't have a job, do you?

WILLIE: Not my fault the army can't build a levee.

MATTIE: You telling me you had a job before the flood?

WILLIE: Yeah, woman, I had a job . . . sort of . . . when they needed me.

MATTIE: People don't call that a job, Clarence. People call that unemployed.

WILLIE: Why you got to be this way with me? (*Turning to BEAU.*) Especially in front of strangers.

MATTIE: This is Beau Harlan, my tenant.

WILLIE: Tenant? Him? I thought he was doing some work on your place or something.

MATTIE: And this is Clarence Williams, an old acquaintance.

WILLIE: Willie. Willie Williams. (*To MATTIE.*) Why you got to be calling me Clarence? You know that's not what I go by now.

MATTIE: Maybe Clarence isn't what you go by, but Clarence is what you is. (*Pause.*) And what you always will be, far as I'm concerned.

WILLIE: She cold, ain't she, Beau? Standing outside in the middle of January, man, she could make an icicle shiver.

BEAU: I wouldn't know about any of that. I just rent is all, Clarence.

WILLIE: It's Willie. Willie Williams. (*To MATTIE.*) You see? Now you got him doing it, too.

MATTIE: What you doing over here, anyway?

WILLIE: Opportunity come along I want to share with my friends.

MATTIE: I told you last time, I'm not lending you any money.

WILLIE: I don't need your money. I come by to see your father. He home?

MATTIE: Only money he got left is what I give him. And he ain't getting a penny out of me for one of your damn fool schemes.

WILLIE: Your daddy home, woman, or not?

MATTIE: Long as there's food in the kitchen, he's home, all right. (*Calling as she opens the door.*) Daddy.

(*MATTIE enters her side of the house.*)

WILLIE: So you Mattie's new tenant, huh, Beau?

BEAU: Lost our house over in Gentilly.

WILLIE: What you doing in this neighborhood? You a long way from home.

BEAU: Got to live somewhere—and not many places I can afford.

WILLIE: Why? What you do?

BEAU: Carpentry.

WILLIE: Shit, I'd 've thought everybody and his brother'd be looking for a carpenter, way things are. You must be making money hand over fist.

BEAU: You'd think so, but until somebody gets some insurance money, something from the government, there aren't many can afford a carpenter to fix their house.

WILLIE: Me, I'm looking into some entrepreneurial opportunities. That's what I want to talk to Dex about. (*Pause.*) But look here, Beau, you interested in investing in a can't-miss business? Easy money, let me tell you.

BEAU: Only thing I'm looking to invest in is some sheetrock for my house.

WILLIE: I might be able to hook you up with some of that sheetrock—and not for what you be paying at Home Depot, neither. Or maybe you could use some copper tubing. Cheap, I'm talking about.

BEAU (*unlocking his door*): Well, it'll be awhile before I'm in a position to start buying building supplies.

DEX (*coming out onto the porch*): Hey, Willie, long time, no see. Where you been, boy?

BEAU: Evening, Mr. Godchaux.

DEX (*gruffly*): Evening.

WILLIE (*to BEAU as he enters his side of the house*): Don't you forget me, you ready to start work. I can get you anything you need.

BEAU: I'll keep that in mind, Clarence.

WILLIE: Willie, man. It's Willie.

BEAU (*closing his door*): Right. You take it easy, Willie.

WILLIE: Why y'all want to rent to some white man can't even remember my name?

DEX: Think it's me? Just more of Mattie's foolishness. You know how the girl gets.

WILLIE: If anybody knows, I'm the one.

DEX: Well, it's not as if you didn't give her reason to throw your ass out.

WILLIE: Nothing but a misunderstanding, all that was. But you think the woman ever heard of second chances? Shit. And you wonder why I never come around.

DEX: Well, Willie, between the two of us, maybe we could change her mind about you. I hate to see my daughter all alone like she is.

WILLIE (*failing to see Mattie coming back onto the porch*): It couldn't be any plainer, Dex, you ask me. That's a woman needs a man.

MATTIE: And you think you that man?

WILLIE: Oh, Mattie, didn't see you standing there.

MATTIE: I'm here all right. Making sure you don't run off my tenant somehow.

WILLIE: What you got that raggedy ass white man living in your house for, anyway?

MATTIE: That raggedy ass white man pays his rent on time, just like he said he would. When you ever keep any promises you made?

WILLIE: Water under the bridge, that's how you got to think about the past, girl. It's the here and now, only thing really matters. (*With a big grin.*) And here I am.

MATTIE: What you know about the past, huh, Clarence? You can't even remember your own name.

(*MATTIE exits. DEX looks at WILLIE, shakes his head, and exits. Lights fade.*)

(*BEAU plays the guitar in his kitchen on a Sunday morning. A cup of coffee is on the table.*)

BEAU (*singing with a bluegrass twang*):

> *My home's across the Smoky Mountains,*
> *My home's across the Smoky Mountains,*
> *My home's across the Smoky Mountains,*
> *And I 'spect I'll never see you anymore.*
>
> *How can I keep from crying,*
> *How can I keep from crying,*
> *How can I keep from crying,*
> *For I 'spect I'll never see you anymore.*
>
> *My home's across the Smoky Mountains—*

(*BEAU is interrupted by knocking at the offstage front door. He goes to open the door.*)

DEX (*following BEAU back into the kitchen*): You killing a dog or something? That what's going on over here?
BEAU: No, sir, Mr. Godchaux, I'm just singing is all.

(*He holds up his guitar as proof.*)

DEX: Singing? That your idea of music, that . . . that yelping I heard.

BEAU: My father taught me the song when I was a boy.

DEX: And he the one told you that's what singing sounds like?

BEAU: People said he had a fine voice, my father.

DEX: And where your daddy come from with this fine voice of his?

BEAU: Arkansas.

DEX: Arkansas? You think them hillbillies know the first thing about music? Shit. Those people think you clang two spoons together, you playing an instrument.

BEAU: Well, look, I didn't mean to bother you with my guitar. I figured a Sunday morning, you and your daughter'd be at church.

DEX: Mattie, she at church, all right. But me, I done give up on it.

BEAU: Same for me.

DEX: Since the flood, you mean?

BEAU: Since I lose my wife.

DEX: Your wife? (*Pauses, then takes a seat.*) Yeah, that was the end of church-going for me, too. Once my Lucille died.

BEAU (*pouring DEX a cup of coffee*): A while ago?

DEX: Not so long. Nine years.

BEAU: Nine years? That's nearly half my whole married life.

DEX: Don't feel like long to me. Feel like last night I come home from work and find her lying there on the floor.

BEAU: You lose somebody you love, it's always just yesterday it happened.

DEX: We grew up together, Lucille and me. Two little children running 'round the neighborhood, and it never crossing my mind that little Jackson gal down the block gonna be my wife someday.

BEAU: It sneaks up on you, don't it, realizing you in love with somebody.

DEX: Sometimes. And sometimes it hits you right between the eyes like a ten-pound sledgehammer.

BEAU: Me, no. Nothing sudden about it. No sledgehammer. More like, I don't know, the tide coming in, I guess. And me standing

there soaking wet, wondering where the hell all this water
come from.
DEX: It'll do that, love. Drench you to the bone before you even
notice it's raining.

(*Pause.*)

So all you know is hillbilly songs?
BEAU: Guess so.
DEX: Well, I probably know one or two of those.

(*Either picking up the guitar to play it himself or nodding for
BEAU to play it.*)

How 'bout "Goodnight, Irene"?

(*After some strumming, he starts to sing.*)

> *Sometimes I live in the country,*
> *And sometimes I live in town,*
> *And sometimes I take a great notion*
> *To jump into the river and drown.*

DEX and BEAU:

> *Goodnight, Irene, Irene,*
> *Goodnight, Irene,*
> *Goodnight, Irene, goodnight, Irene,*
> *I'll see you in my dreams.*

DEX:

> *Last Saturday night I got married,*
> *Me and my wife settled down,*
> *Now me and my wife are parted,*
> *Gonna take a little stroll downtown.*

DEX and BEAU:

> *Goodnight, Irene, Irene,*
> *Goodnight, Irene,*
> *Goodnight, Irene, goodnight, Irene,*
> *I'll see you in my dreams.*

(The guitar keeps playing as lights fade.)

SCENE 5

*(The front porch of the shotgun. Noon on a weekday. DEX is
sitting on the porch while WILLIE paces, obviously upset and
perhaps sipping from a bottle in a brown paper bag.)*

WILLIE: You hear what the mayor say on Marvin Luther King's
   birthday?

DEX: Martin. *(Pause.) Martin* Luther King, fool.

WILLIE: Yeah, man, Martin Luther King. That's what I said.

DEX: No, you didn't. You said Marvin Luther King. You don't even
   know Reverend King's first name, do you, Clarence?

WILLIE: Willie, Dex. I go by Willie now.

DEX: You expect me to get your name right, then you better go to
   work on Dr. King's name.

WILLIE: Yeah, OK. Martin. Martin Luther King.

DEX: Doctor Martin Luther King, Junior.

WILLIE: Yeah, I got it, but look, Dex. You hear what the mayor
   say? Say God meant this to be a chocolate city, but those white
   people Uptown, they don't want black folks ever going home
   again.

DEX: You really think those people on St. Charles Avenue give a
   good goddamn whether I get back in my house on Tennessee
   Street or not? Shit. Probably couldn't even find the Lower
   Ninth Ward, they went looking for it. Only thing they care
   about, those people, we don't move in next door to them.

WILLIE: I'm telling you, the mayor say they want us out of New Orleans for good. The mayor, man. Think he gonna make some shit up like that, then say it on the TV?

DEX: Who the hell you think put him in office? Those white folks Uptown you so worried about, they the ones made him mayor in the first place.

WILLIE: Just proves my point, man. He knows those people. So he say it, it's got to be true. (*DEX gives him a skeptical look.*) You think I'm crazy, but with everything the way it is now, they see their chance to finally get rid of us, take the city back. Look right here, next door to you and Mattie, who you got living?

DEX: That wasn't my doing.

WILLIE: They taking over, man. All those dogs and fire hoses and everything else Dr. King went through, we gonna lose everything he fought for. You watch. They been lying in wait for a chance like this. Why you think they killed him?

DEX: Don't you forget, boy, I was there at the beginning.

WILLIE: I hear you.

DEX: The bullshit we had to put up with. You and Mattie was little, they still had a sign on the window of that laundry Uptown: "No coloreds. Maids in uniform excepted."

WILLIE: So it's OK, we bringing white folk's things to wash. Just not our own.

DEX: Guess their customers didn't want their clothes mixing with colored people's clothes.

WILLIE: So that's what it means, those signs they got up at the Laundromat I go.

DEX: What signs?

WILLIE (*with a sly smile*): You know, the ones they got over the washing machines. "Do not mix whites and coloreds in the same load."

DEX: It ain't a thing to joke about, boy.

WILLIE: Anyway, it's fine by me. I don't want my clothes mixing with theirs, neither. My granddaddy used to say those people smell like dogs, their hair gets wet. And it gets all up in their clothes, the smell.

DEX: What the hell foolishness you talking about now?

WILLIE: White people. You know how they smell, they get wet.

DEX: Jesus, Clarence, you absolutely hopeless, you know that?

WILLIE: I'm just saying, you wouldn't want to be sitting next to one on the bus, it's been raining. (*Pause.*) And I already told you, it's Willie, my name.

DEX: Call yourself anything you want to, boy, I still spell it "F-O-O-L" in my book.

WILLIE: Chew on my ass all you want, that don't change what's going on around here.

DEX: Just you sound the fool talking the way you do. White people smell like dogs, they get wet. Where you come up with foolishness like that?

WILLIE: Shit, Dex, everybody know it's true. Just like what the mayor say about them wanting to get rid of us.

DEX: Well, I don't trust them anymore than you do, but I don't trust that mayor of yours, neither.

WILLIE: Wait a few months and see he's not right.

DEX: Wait a few months and see he don't get himself reelected with all his talk about this chocolate city of his.

WILLIE: Better him than some white man.

DEX: So he's gonna save us from this big conspiracy white folks got, huh?

WILLIE: Shit, even with him, what chance we got against people like that, those people Uptown?

DEX: What chance you think we had back in the day, boy? Us up against the fire hoses and billy clubs and dogs.

WILLIE: Man, it was a different time. They learned their lesson, those people. They don't make the same mistakes they used to make—not in front of a TV camera anyway.

DEX: No, it don't show up on the evening news anymore, what they do.

WILLIE: But they still do, don't they?

DEX: Yeah, boy, they still do. Down on St. Charles Avenue, who they got on top that big white column all the streetcars have to go around?

WILLIE: Robert E. Lee, you mean?

DEX: Think they ever gonna pull down that statue of Robert E. Lee? General fought a war to keep us slaves.

WILLIE: Tear down Lee Circle?

DEX: But what you think they saying with a statue like that?

(*Pause.*)

WILLIE: Don't forget your place, nigger.

DEX: Maybe you not such a fool after all, Willie.

(*Lights fade.*)

SCENE 6

(*BEAU is drying dishes as EUGENE does his homework at the kitchen table.*)

BEAU: So how's school going? Your teachers OK?

EUGENE: They all right.

BEAU: And you start making friends yet?

EUGENE: Oh yeah, lots of friends.

BEAU: Nobody lay a hand on you, have they?

EUGENE: Not yet.

BEAU: Somebody do, you go talk to your teachers. They'll stop it.

EUGENE: I can take care of myself. And I can't, I got a little friend named Barlow to give me a hand.

(*He pulls out a large Barlow knife from his pocket and opens it.*)

BEAU: Where the hell you get that?

EUGENE: It was Grandpa's. He gave it to me the birthday before he died.

BEAU: And you take that to school?

EUGENE: My future friends there got worse than knives in their backpacks.

BEAU: The police stop you, you any idea the trouble you'd be in, they found it on you?

EUGENE: What police? When they saw the storm coming, they all ran off to Houston in those Cadillacs they stole.

BEAU: Boy, you just begging for grief with that in your pocket. Give it here.

EUGENE: You gonna leave me defenseless at that school you making me go?

BEAU: You're safer without it. You just don't know.

EUGENE: And you do, huh? All I got to do is put my trust in you, and I'll be fine. (*Pause.*) Just like Mama did.

BEAU: Think it's been easy on me, what happened?

EUGENE: I think listening to you could get a person killed. Wouldn't be the first time I seen it happen.

BEAU: You're not walking out of this house with that knife in your pocket.

EUGENE: You want to try and take it away from me?

BEAU: No, you're gonna hand it over.

EUGENE: The hell I am.

BEAU: Boy—

EUGENE: I'm done listening to you.

BEAU: I'll have that knife right now.

(*BEAU holds out his hand.*)

EUGENE (*holding up the open knife*): I've had this knife in my pocket since the day the storm hit. And this the first you even know about it. All this time, and I haven't gotten into any trouble yet.

BEAU: I'll have the knife.

EUGENE: Think I'm afraid of you?

(*BEAU stares him down.*)

But I don't care. You want my knife so bad, here—take it.

(*EUGENE folds the knife and puts it on the table.*)

BEAU: I find out you taking anything but books to school, we'll see whether you got reason to be afraid.

EUGENE (*gathering up his books from the table and approaching BEAU*): Yeah, we'll just have to see whether somebody's got reason to be afraid.

(*He pushes past BEAU toward the front room.*)

I got homework to finish.

(*EUGENE exits to the front room. BEAU sits down at the kitchen table, opens the knife, stares at the blade, then snaps it shut. Lights fade.*)

(Late afternoon on the front porch of the shotgun. MATTIE is sitting on the steps sorting beans in a bowl and flicking away the tiny stones she finds among the beans. BEAU opens his front door and steps out onto the porch.)

MATTIE: Good afternoon.

BEAU: Oh, afternoon, Miss Godchaux. I didn't see you sitting there.

MATTIE: The days are getting longer. Guess winter's nearly done.

BEAU: I was just checking on my boy. Should have been home by now.

MATTIE: Still at school?

BEAU: They're having tryouts for the football team before spring training starts.

MATTIE: It's hard going to a new school.

BEAU: Yes, ma'am. He's not having an easy time of it.

MATTIE: You know, Mr. Harlan, don't you think it's about time we start calling each other by our first names? We been neighbors over a month now.

BEAU: Yes, ma'am, I suppose it is.

MATTIE (*laughing*): Not "ma'am." "Mattie."

BEAU: And "Beau." (*Pause.*) Kind of old-fashioned. It was my mother's father's name.

MATTIE: No, I like it. Beau. Suits you.

BEAU: And your name's short for—what?—Mathilda?

MATTIE: Mathilda? (*Looking at him as if horrified at the idea.*)
No, just Mattie. Don't know where they got it. Asked my father
once. Said he didn't know either how I come by my name.
(*Pause.*) Such a tease, that man.

BEAU: Suits you, too. (*Pause.*) So what you doing, Mattie?

MATTIE: Sorting beans. You never picked out stones from beans?

BEAU: No, ma'am. I mean, no, Mattie, never did. My mama handled
all the cooking I was a boy. Then Audrey, well, she did all that
once we got married.

MATTIE: And in between?

BEAU: Wasn't any in between. Graduated high school one week,
got married the next.

MATTIE: High-school sweethearts?

BEAU: That's what everybody called us. But it seemed like I was
born knowing her.

MATTIE: Same for Mama and Daddy. Grew up together.

BEAU: Mr. Godchaux told me.

MATTIE: My father talked to you about that?

BEAU: One Sunday morning. Lucille, he said her name was, wasn't
it, your mother?

MATTIE: That's right. I'm just surprised to hear you say he told
you about Mama. Doesn't bring her name up all that much
with other people.

BEAU: Yeah, well, we got to talking about what it's like to lose
somebody you love.

MATTIE: Daddy mentioned you lost your wife.

BEAU: Audrey.

MATTIE: In the hurricane?

WILLIE (*entering, a bit dressed up*): Hope I'm not late for dinner.

MATTIE: Dinner? Why, where you think you eating?

WILLIE: Dex invited me the other day.

MATTIE: He didn't say nothing to me.

WILLIE: Must've slipped his mind, I guess.

MATTIE: Yeah, his mind's getting more slippery hour by hour,
that man.

WILLIE: You ain't gonna deny a guest your father's hospitality, are you?

MATTIE: You telling me my father actually thought I'd have you over here to dinner?

WILLIE: Said he thought it might be a chance for us to talk, the three of us. Go ask him, you don't believe me.

MATTIE: Just what I'm fixing to do, Clarence.

(*She exits.*)

WILLIE (*to BEAU*): So you still here, huh?

BEAU: Got nowhere else to go.

WILLIE: You see the mayor on the TV?

BEAU: On Martin Luther King's birthday, you mean?

WILLIE: Doctor Martin Luther King Junior's birthday, yeah. So what you say, Beau? Think he's right God meant New Orleans to be a chocolate city?

BEAU: Tell you the truth, I haven't given it much thought, Clarence.

WILLIE: It's Willie, my name.

BEAU: Right, Willie. Like I say, haven't given it much thought what flavor we supposed to be.

WILLIE: Well, think about it now. This gonna be a chocolate city or not?

BEAU: You swing by the parking lot of Home Depot in the morning, with all the Mexicans looking for work, I wouldn't be surprised we wind up some kind of refried bean city before we're done.

WILLIE: Don't you worry about that. The mayor already say he ain't gonna stand by and let Mexicans overrun the place.

BEAU: And what's he gonna do about all the damn Texans we got here now. And Georgians? And all those contractors and roofers from Florida come over here?

WILLIE: That's not what I'm asking you, man.

BEAU (*beginning to stiffen*): Well, what are you asking, Willie?

WILLIE: I got to spell it out for you?

BEAU: You asking whether I want this place to go back the way it was? (*Slight pause.*) Can't say I do.

WILLIE: So the mayor's right you white people looking to take things back.

BEAU: The schools we had, the housing projects, the crime, the politicians stealing us blind. That's what God meant for us?

WILLIE: White man do that, nobody open their mouth. Black man come along, all of a sudden, shit, we got to do something about all this corruption dragging us down.

BEAU: Not me. I say put 'em all in prison. Black, white, Mexican— they break the law, lock 'em up.

WILLIE: Depends on whose law you talking about, don't it?

BEAU: The law's the law.

WILLIE (*laughing*): Man, you wouldn't last ten minutes somebody turn your ass chocolate.

MATTIE (*entering*): My father's getting dressed to take you out to dinner. Says he'll meet you over at Jayjay's in fifteen minutes.

WILLIE: You won't even have me at your table?

MATTIE: And what would I serve you if I did? You don't see me out here cleaning beans?

WILLIE: Beans? You know how long they take to cook? You ain't gonna eat till midnight, you make beans.

MATTIE: Nobody told me you were coming over. And I just got home a little while ago.

WILLIE: My mama ain't never put beans on the stove the same night we ate them. That's weekend cooking, making beans.

MATTIE: Well, next weekend I get finished buying the groceries, washing the clothes, filling up the car with gas, and paying all the bills, I'll try to remember to put a pot of beans on the fire, too, case you decide to stop by for dinner some night after work. (*Pause.*) My work, I mean.

WILLIE: You don't have to get all high and mighty with me just 'cause you got a job, woman.

MATTIE: Well, I got a job for you. Go see can you find two barstools together at Jayjay's. Wouldn't want my daddy to have to eat standing up.

WILLIE: Maybe you want to come along, too? They got tables over there, you know.

MATTIE: I got beans to cook, Clarence.

WILLIE: Woman, you got a heart as hard as them stones you tossing away.

(*Willie exits.*)

MATTIE: As if I ain't got enough to do, I'm supposed to feed that boy, too.

BEAU: I knew how to cook, I'd invite you over tonight. But all I got's a poor chicken drying out in the oven for me and Gene.

MATTIE (*laughing*): Well, come over here and let me at least teach you how to sort stones from beans.

(*BEAU takes a seat beside MATTIE on the steps and scoops up a handful of beans.*)

BEAU: You know just now when you were talking about filling up your car at the service station every weekend, made me think of something I overheard the other day. I'm getting gas for the truck, and I hear a man on the other side of the pump talking on his phone. Insurance agent, I guess he was. "Yes, ma'am," he says, "we'll come tow your flooded car away. But you got to get the car off the roof of the house yourself."

MATTIE (*laughing*): You making that up.

BEAU: God's honest truth, that's what the man said. "You got to get the car off the roof of the house yourself."

(*Lights fade as they laugh together.*)

(BEAU plays the guitar in his kitchen at night. A half-empty glass and a bottle of bourbon sit on the table. He's been drinking.)

BEAU (*singing with deep feeling*):

> My home's across the Smoky Mountains,
> My home's across the Smoky Mountains,
> My home's across the Smoky Mountains,
> And I 'spect I'll never see you anymore.
>
> How can I keep from crying—

(BEAU is interrupted by knocking at the front door. He goes to open the door and returns with MATTIE.)

MATTIE: I was sitting in my kitchen and heard the music coming through the wall.

BEAU: Guess I was singing louder than I thought. Your father send you over to complain?

MATTIE: No, Friday nights Daddy plays cards at his cousin's house across the river. Be there all night, most likely. (*Pause.*) Didn't know you could sing.

BEAU: When we first moved in, your father let me know he didn't much care for my singing. My son, neither. Only time I sing's when he's not here.

MATTIE: Really? 'Cause it was lovely, the song. Never heard it before, though.

BEAU: First time I sang it to her, Audrey decided that would be our song.

(*Silence.*)

You care to sit down?

MATTIE (*sitting*): So where's your boy?

BEAU: Football practice—he should've been home by now, though. I keep calling, but he don't answer his phone.

MATTIE: Maybe the boys went out together afterward. You know how teammates are.

BEAU: If he made the team. The coaches were going to announce their final cuts tonight. He didn't think he had much chance against the players they already got.

MATTIE: Then maybe he's gone off with his old friends.

BEAU: They all living somewhere else for now. (*Pause.*) I worry 'cause the boy's so angry all the time.

MATTIE: A lot of people are these days.

BEAU: I mean he's mad at me.

MATTIE: You?

BEAU: I'm the one decided we wouldn't evacuate.

MATTIE: You not the only one chose to stay.

BEAU: He says his mother'd still be alive, we'd left the day before the storm. (*Pause.*) And he's not wrong.

(*Silence.*)

MATTIE (*picking up the bottle of bourbon*): You got another glass?

BEAU: Oh, I'm sorry. Should have asked when you come in.

(*He puts a glass on the table for her; she fills it and then refills his glass. They drink throughout the rest of the scene.*)

MATTIE: You know, I had a child once, too . . . Yolanda. Sweetest little thing you ever saw. And her grandpa thought she'd hung the moon, that girl.

BEAU: What happened?

MATTIE: Sickle cell anemia. You know about that?

BEAU: I know it hits you all real hard, black people.

MATTIE: In the beginning, you can't tell anything is wrong. Yolanda was four or five months old when Daddy noticed it, the way her hands and feet looked swollen all the time. We took her to the doctor, he says, yeah, she's got them, all right, sickle cells. And already by then her spleen was hurt. It would have been all right we'd had more time, she'd gotten bigger, but that winter she come down with pneumonia. (*Pause.*) And that was that.

BEAU: I'm so sorry.

MATTIE: In the beginning, Clarence—he was the father—

BEAU: You mean Willie, that fellow always comes by here? He don't seem your type.

MATTIE: He was different then, that boy. When we first found out, Clarence couldn't have been any sweeter. Coming by my parents' house all the time, bringing presents for the baby— you know, little things.

BEAU: You were living with your parents?

MATTIE: Still in high school, the both of us. But when the baby died, something happened. Me, it made me grow up quick, I think. Clarence, though, it hit him just the opposite. Frightened him off of growing up, I guess. He never really got over it. I see him on the corner now, it's like he hasn't changed in twenty years.

BEAU: Well, now he's changed his name at least.

MATTIE: This foolishness about his name, it's just what I'm saying. "Willie Williams?" That's not his name. That never was his name. It's just another way of sliding past, that's all it is.

(*His cell phone rings, and BEAU answers it.*)

BEAU (*on the phone*): Where the hell you been? I'm sitting here
    worried sick. (*Pause.*) I'm sorry to hear that, son. (*Pause.*)
    Don't talk like that. And I don't ever want to hear that word
    come out your mouth again. I'm sure the coaches never let that
    enter into it. (*Pause.*) Yeah, I know how much you wanted to.
    (*Pause.*) Robbie? How'd you find him? (*Pause.*) He come all the
    way over here to pick you up? (*Pause.*) Where's that? (*Pause.*)
    The whole night? You sure it's all right with Robbie's parents?
    Those trailers don't have much room inside. (*Pause.*) OK, I'll
    come get you in the morning. (*Pause.*) Hey, and look, Gene,
    you be careful, OK? (*Pause.*) Yeah, I know you are. Just be
    careful, you hear?

(*BEAU hangs up the phone.*)

He didn't make the team.
MATTIE: I figured from what you said.
BEAU: He's spending the night with a friend from his old school.
MATTIE: That's good. Take his mind off his disappointment.
BEAU: I just don't like him running around at night with all the
    streets deserted, the lights out everywhere.
MATTIE: He'll be OK. Apart from all the looting, there's hardly any
    crime to speak of.
BEAU: Yeah, maybe the city will come out of this a brand-new place.
MATTIE: And us all brand-new people, huh?

(*Pause.*)

BEAU: You really think a person ever changes?
MATTIE: I don't know. You get to an age when you think it's all
    settled, don't you? The way I am, it's fixed for life.
BEAU: One thing I learned the last few months, nothing stays fixed
    for good.
MATTIE: I guess after what you been through, that's something
    you know all about.

(*Silence.*)

BEAU: Tell you, I had no idea a person could be so all alone. Even
though the boy's been with me every night. (*Pause.*) I never
knew they got so many different ways to be lonesome.
MATTIE: Oh yeah. Me, I keep finding new ways to be lonely, seems
like all the time.
BEAU: You think you know all the ways it sneaks up on you,
remembering what it was that happened. Then some tiny thing
you never even thought about before—the one glass on the
table just now, for instance—and there it is, the wound torn
open all over again, and just as raw and jagged as it started off.
MATTIE: You got an open wound, the world is full of salt.
BEAU: You got an open wound, the world's got worse than salt.

(*Silence.*)

MATTIE: You never did tell me how she died, your wife.

(*Pause.*)

I'm sorry. If you don't want to talk about it—
BEAU: No, it's all right. She died just after the storm. About two
weeks later in Baton Rouge.
MATTIE: Baton Rouge?
BEAU: In the hospital. (*Pause.*) We stayed through the storm, me
and Audrey and Gene. It passes by, and nothing to show for it.
I'm already thinking I'll be back at work the next morning, lose
just the one day's wages—until we see the water coming down
the street from both directions.
MATTIE: Even if somebody'd said so, who'd 've believed them, the
levees all crumbling?
BEAU: Next thing we know, we're in the attic with water up around
our ankles and still getting deeper. My daddy, he gave us an
ax for a housewarming present. Said keep it in the attic case

you ever need it. Everybody took it as a joke, but Daddy tells me before the party's over, just put it up the attic like I said. It's not such an easy thing, though, swinging an ax upside down against the roof in a low attic. That's three-quarter inch plywood, roofing. The water's everywhere and still coming. I hit the wood false, and the ax slips out of my hands. So I reach down to pick it up, and my arm's up to the elbow in water before I find it in the dark up there. I tell you, I swung the ax like John Henry after that—and finally it gives way, the plywood. I chop a hole in the roof, and the three of us, we shimmy up out of there. Plywood, though, it don't cut clean with an ax. The hole's jagged as a broken window. We all get cut up pretty good coming out onto the roof, Audrey worst of all. (*Pause.*) Next day, man come by in a flatboat just before noon, offers to take us to the overpass of the interstate, we want. Says you can't believe the way it looks, everywhere he's been so far. (*Pause.*) Thing is, the gutter's all torn loose somehow, and everything floated to the surface, it's trapped up there between the gutter and where we are. So the boat can't get close enough to tie up to our roof. "Swim for it," he says, the man. I mean, we only talking fifteen, maybe twenty feet tops, we got to swim—and he drags us up into the boat fast as he can once we get there. But Audrey's got this wide-open gash runs down her thigh, and she won't get in the boat till Gene goes first. She's hanging on the gunnel, waiting her turn in all that filthy water. I'm trying to shoulder the boy up over the side, and somehow Audrey's hand slips. When she comes up, she's choking, spitting out the water.

MATTIE: And what was in that water, huh?

BEAU: They still don't know. The doctors told me we had two hundred thousand cars submerged. So gasoline, they said, and all those chemicals and poisons people got around the house and rivers of raw sewage floating down the street. The doctors said they didn't know what the hell they were dealing with.

MATTIE: And your wife with an open wound in all that mess.

BEAU: And all the water she swallowed, too. The next day it's got to be a hundred degrees on that overpass when they finally put us in a bus to Baton Rouge. Audrey, though, she's shivering with fever. I tell the driver take us to a hospital. But no, he says, he's got his orders. They drop us off at some basketball gymnasium and leave us there. I start looking for a doctor, but there's none that I can find. So we wait a bit, see whether the fever maybe breaks. Next morning, she's looking better. The worst is over, I think. The next few days, she's weak but not so hot. I tell her we ought to see a doctor. She says it's just the sun from a day on the roof and another on the overpass. By the weekend, I think she's got it licked. Then Sunday night the fever, it comes roaring back. They take her to the hospital. (*Pause.*) Audrey, she don't get better, she don't get worse. Then one night someone comes wakes me up. Says there's a police car waiting to take me and Gene to the hospital. That's all they know, but hurry up they say. (*Pause.*) We get there, and the infection, they can't control it anymore. It's eating her alive, they say. And nothing left they haven't tried already. I touch her, and she's burning up. (*Pause.*) She didn't last the night.

(*Silence as BEAU weeps. MATTIE crosses to BEAU and hesitantly puts her arm around his shoulders to comfort him.*)

All the years we were together, my Audrey never once let me eat breakfast by myself. Gets up with me 5:30 every morning. When Gene's a little baby and she's up all night with him, I tell her, "You sleep, I'll fix me something for myself." She say, "Don't you worry, I'll go back to bed after you leave for work." Never once let me eat breakfast alone, that girl.

(*BEAU starts to sob. MATTIE pulls him closer.*)

MATTIE: It's all right, baby. It's gonna be all right.

(*She hugs him. Perhaps BEAU looks up into MATTIE's face. Blackout.*)

ACT II

SCENE 1

(*The middle of the night. Sounds of the front door being opened and the crash of furniture as a very drunken EUGENE stumbles into the dark kitchen and collapses, giggling, at the table. BEAU, in just his underwear, enters from the bedroom door and flips on the light. The bottle and two glasses are still on the table. EUGENE reacts to the light by covering his eyes.*)

BEAU: What the hell's going on in here?

EUGENE: Nothing.

BEAU: You drunk?

EUGENE: What if I am?

BEAU: You told me you were spending the night at Robbie's.

EUGENE: It's all so small inside those trailers. They got these kind of shelves you supposed to sleep on, but I didn't fit.

BEAU: You should've called. I'd 've come and got you.

EUGENE: Robbie said he'd run me home. We stopped off on the way, though.

BEAU: At a bar? Who the hell would sell liquor to boys your age?

EUGENE: Think anybody in this city's checking you old enough for what you want?

BEAU: And you let Robbie drive back home across the bridge in this condition?

EUGENE: He didn't drink so much as me.

BEAU (*shaking his head*): We'll talk in the morning about all this. You go get some sleep.

119

EUGENE: I'm not sleeping on that sofa one more night. You think it's so damn comfortable, you go sleep on it.

BEAU: Get in the living room, and stop all this foolishness.

EUGENE: What I'm gonna stop is listening to you anymore. I seen where that leads.

BEAU: We're not having this conversation with you drunk. Now go get on that sofa like I said.

EUGENE (*trying to barge past BEAU into the bedroom*): I told you I'm sleeping in a bed tonight.

BEAU (*stopping EUGENE*): And I say you're not.

EUGENE (*taking a wild swing at BEAU*): The hell you say.

(*BEAU wraps EUGENE in a bear hug, and they struggle.*)

MATTIE (*entering from the bedroom, wearing just BEAU's shirt*): Let him sleep in the bed if he wants to, Beau.

(*BEAU releases EUGENE.*)

EUGENE: What's she doing here?

BEAU: You don't understand, Gene.

EUGENE: Oh, I understand all right. Mama's dead not five months, and you and that black—

BEAU: One more word, so help me, and I'll—

EUGENE: You'll what? Think after what you done, you got the right to tell me anything.

MATTIE: Your father . . . he misses your mama something terrible.

EUGENE: Just who the hell you think killed my mama?

MATTIE (*approaching EUGENE*): That wasn't your father, Eugene. You want to blame somebody, blame the men built that worthless levee by your house.

(*Mattie tries to put her arm around EUGENE's shoulders.*)

EUGENE (*twisting away*): Don't you touch me. Don't you dare touch me.

BEAU: Gene, you got to try to understand—
EUGENE: I understand all right. I understand I come home
after getting cut from the football team and find you in bed
screwing that nigger.

(*BEAU slaps EUGENE.*)

BEAU: Don't you ever use that word in my house.
EUGENE: This ain't your house. This house is hers. You lost our
house for us just like you lost Mama.
BEAU: Gene—
EUGENE: Don't talk to me. (*He starts to exit.*) And don't come
looking for me, neither. I'm not sleeping in this house tonight.

(*EUGENE exits, slamming the front door.*)

BEAU: I'm sorry you had to hear that.
MATTIE: Not the first time somebody called me "nigger."
BEAU: He doesn't mean it. Before his mother died, he never was
anything like this.
MATTIE: The boy's got nobody else to blame but you for how he feels.
BEAU: Me and now probably you, too.
MATTIE: Maybe I better go in case he comes home later on tonight.
BEAU (*sitting down at the kitchen table*): Yeah, he's got no place to
sleep but the bed of my truck out front. I'll let him cool off and
go get him in a little while.
MATTIE (*joining BEAU at the table*): I'm sorry he came in on us,
Beau, but I don't regret what we done.
BEAU: No, you got nothing to regret. If anybody's guilty for what
went on tonight, it's me. You were just being kind, that's all.
Taking pity.
MATTIE: This didn't have a thing to do with feeling sorry for
anybody but myself.

(*Pause.*)

BEAU (*rubbing his face*): I haven't slept so deep since before the
    flood.
MATTIE: Well, that don't sound like somebody guilty of anything
    to me. (*Pause.*) What we done tonight, it ain't adultery.
BEAU: Sure feels a lot like that must feel.
MATTIE: Beau, you not a married man no more.

(*Pause.*)

BEAU: I wasn't so damn tired, this would all be easier. The middle
    of the night, my eyes still shut tight, I'm all of a sudden wide
    awake, worried about some problem never even occurred to
    me till now.
MATTIE: You can't fall back asleep?
BEAU: I try to go to sleep again, it never works. I lie there waiting
    for the alarm to ring, wide awake for hours in the dark.
MATTIE: But you slept all right tonight—at least until your boy
    came home. Like a dead man lying there, you slept.
BEAU: Wouldn't surprise me someone come along and say that's
    what's wrong with me. "Mister, you dead and just don't know
    it. You been dead a good five months by now."
MATTIE: Or maybe you just deep asleep, and only a kiss will wake
    you up.
BEAU: You talking fairy tales.
MATTIE: And this ain't that? Some fairy tale where everybody's
    cursed and no one's there to break the spell.
BEAU: But you and me, we not some kids believe in fairy tales. So
    what we gonna do, Mattie? What we gonna do?

(*Lights fade.*)

SCENE 2

(*The front porch of the shotgun the next morning. DEX is knocking on MATTIE's door while WILLIE waits on the steps. They have been drinking.*)

DEX: Open up, Mattie. (*He knocks again.*) You in there, girl?

WILLIE: You think she's all right, Dex? Think something might have happened to her?

MATTIE (*opening the door, half awake*): Why you making such a racket? How come you didn't just use your key?

DEX: Lost it, I guess, or forgot it last night when I got dressed. I don't know.

(*MATTIE steps onto the porch, rubbing her eyes and yawning.*)

MATTIE: And what you got Clarence with you for?

WILLIE: Someone had to go and pick your father up—since nobody could find you all last night.

MATTIE: What's he talking about?

DEX: I call you two or three times last night to come over there, but you ain't never picked up the phone.

MATTIE: You always stay at your cousin's house on Friday nights. Why'd you want to come back home, anyway?

DEX: Yeah, well, I wasn't getting the cards I was looking for and ran a little short.

MATTIE: You run through all that money I gave you before you left last night?

DEX: That's why I was calling you. Thought you could bring me over a little more so I could win back what I lost.

MATTIE: You must have been some drunk, thought I'd give you any more money to throw away on cards. No wonder you couldn't dial my number straight.

WILLIE: Dex didn't have no trouble dialing me.

DEX: Yeah, Willie, he picks up his phone right away and comes across the river to help me out. Stakes me twenty dollars to get back in the game. Not like some ungrateful child begrudges her father a little fun.

MATTIE: So in the end, you win back all my money?

DEX: For a while. Right, Willie? We doing OK for a while.

MATTIE: But when the game was done?

DEX: Why you got to be like this? (*Pause.*) Just had a run of bad luck at the end, that's all. Willie did all right, though, didn't you, boy?

WILLIE: Made forty-eight dollars. Not a bad night's work.

MATTIE: That ain't work, Clarence.

DEX: And . . . I promised the boy you'd pay him back the twenty bucks he lent me.

MATTIE: You know how hard I work for my money?

WILLIE: You got that white man next door paying you his rent.

MATTIE: You leave Beau out of this, you understand, Clarence?

WILLIE: Just saying, it's not like you poverty stricken or something with all that money coming in every month.

DEX: And don't be go changing the subject, girl. Where was you last night when I needed you?

MATTIE: I have my own life to live.

DEX: You went out somewhere on your own?

MATTIE: No. (*Pause.*) I never . . . I never stepped foot off my own property all last night, you have to know. Not my fault you were too drunk to dial a telephone.

DEX: I tell you, girl, I called this house last night.

MATTIE: Where I ever go, huh, Daddy? Home and work and home again, that's my whole damn life. What you think? I got some secret somebody loves me?

WILLIE: Dex knows you got somebody loves you. You just don't love him back.

MATTIE: That man had his chances more than once, and where'd it go? You tell me, Clarence, what did that man do with all the chances I gave him?

WILLIE: Maybe you weren't so angry all the time, it'd be a little easier for a man to love you the way you want.

DEX: You my own daughter, Mattie, but you not the easiest girl to love, I tell you.

MATTIE: What you men want, anyway? I'll tell you what. Somebody makes excuses for every damn thing you do.

DEX: You ever hear your mama talk like this to me?

MATTIE: Well, I guess she was just better at putting up with things I can't put up with.

DEX: Baby, a man's just a man. You can't find a way to love the one loves you, time you done, there won't be nobody left to love.

WILLIE: After a while, Mattie, even true love, it'll burn itself out, there's not somebody stoking the fire now and then.

DEX: The boy knows what he's talking about, girl.

MATTIE: Think I don't see what you're after, Daddy? Marry me off to Clarence here and move in the other side of my shotgun for the rest of your life.

DEX (to WILLIE): I guess my daughter'd rather have me a poor homeless man sleeping on a sofa every night.

WILLIE: What they say in the Bible? (Imitating a preacher.) Sharper than a serpent's tooth, an ungrateful child.

MATTIE: You two fools been out drinking and playing cards all Friday night, and I got to stand on my own porch listening to a sermon from you on Saturday morning? I'm going back to bed.

(*She starts to enter the house.*)

WILLIE: But, Mattie, before you go to sleep if you don't mind, I
could use that twenty dollars I lent your father.

(*MATTIE slams the door behind her as she exits.*)

DEX: You hear what she calls him?

WILLIE: Who?

DEX: Her tenant. Called him "Beau" just now.

WILLIE: Yeah, man, that's his name.

DEX: Not just his name, not the way she said it.

WILLIE: Aw, c'mon, Dex, you don't think . . . ?

DEX: Didn't step foot off my own property all last night, she says.
Wouldn't have to, would she? (*Pause.*) She say anything to you
about her tenant?

WILLIE: You think your daughter confides in me?

DEX: This is all your fault, you know.

WILLIE: Me? What's it got to do with me, what went on last night?
I was playing cards with you.

DEX: Girl has a point about all them second chances she give you.

WILLIE: Think I don't know that? Just . . . it's like, I'm around her,
there ain't no starting fresh with anything. Like far as she's
concerned, when it comes to me, can't nothing ever be any
different than what it's already been.

DEX: Maybe 'cause you don't show her nothing different than what
she already seen.

WILLIE: What's the point, Dex? That daughter of yours gonna cut
me any slack, I do?

DEX: Sounds like you the one thinks can't nothing ever be any
different than what it's already been.

WILLIE: So you side with her then?

DEX: It's just . . . boy, why you play the fool all the time?

WILLIE: Fool? What you talking about, fool?

DEX: Oh, come on, Clarence. I remember you, man, the way you used to be.

WILLIE: Yeah, well, that was a long time ago, Dex.

DEX: You were gonna tear this world up. Had all kinds of ideas what you were gonna do. (*Pause.*) I know I gave you hell, getting Mattie pregnant and all, but tell you the truth, I was glad it wasn't none of them other boys from the neighborhood responsible. I thought of all of Mattie's friends back then, Clarence was the one with the future.

WILLIE: Things don't always turn out the way you want.

DEX: You talking to a machinist, boy. How many times I had a chunk of steel spinning in a lathe, and when I was done, what was left of it but what I wanted?

WILLIE: But sometimes, Dex, it's you wind up the chunk of steel spinning in a lathe.

DEX: So, what, you just gonna go with the flow, man, let the world sweep you away?

WILLIE: What you think I'm doing living over here, this side of the river? Think I'm over here for any other reason but your daughter's sake?

DEX: It ain't enough, boy, you hang around the kitchen table, hoping somebody puts a plate in front of you.

WILLIE: Yeah, I'm getting tired of watching other people eat their full while I go hungry.

DEX: But like my grandma used to say, Clarence, it do go by. And you wait too long, you find everything you waiting for, it done done gone by already.

(*Lights fade.*)

(*DEX follows BEAU into the kitchen from the offstage front door.*)

DEX: My daughter tells me you promised to fix her shed out back.

BEAU: Yes, sir, in exchange for Mattie teaching me how to cook. Y'all provide the materials, and I'll do the work.

DEX: So that's what she's doing over here all the time, huh? Teaching you to cook. (*Pause.*) Well, Mattie says for me to come find out exactly what all you need to do the job. Then I'll have a talk with Willie, see what he can lay his hands on.

BEAU: It won't take much. Two sheets of exterior plywood and a roll of tar paper. Some cedar shakes to tile the roof would look real nice. (*Pause.*) And wouldn't hurt to put new hinges on the door while we're at it.

DEX: The way it is right now, with all the looting going on and everybody thinking they can make off with anything they see, that door could use a lock on it as well.

BEAU: Easy enough to add a buckle for a padlock if you want.

DEX: Not that a padlock would keep them out, they looking to steal something I salvaged from the flood.

BEAU: But it would slow them down at least, a lock.

DEX: Depends on how much violence they willing to do to get the thing they're after. Some people around here, they don't seem to mind how much they destroy to get some little trifle that appeals to them. (*Pause.*) You sure you carpenter enough to fix what's broken?

BEAU: What other kind of carpenter is there?

DEX: The kind that builds from scratch. (*Pause.*) It's one thing to come along and throw up a house on some empty lot. Anybody can learn to do that sort of work. (*Pause.*) But taking something that's already standing and fixing the damage that's been done to it, fix it so nobody can tell it ever had been broken in the first place, now that's the kind of carpenter my daughter needs.

BEAU: I know my trade.

DEX: Maybe so, but I seen things repaired only hide the damage that's been done. You put a little pressure on the patch, you wind up with a bigger hole than what you started with.

BEAU: You won't know there ever was a storm, I get done with fixing what's been hurt.

DEX: That's just exactly what I'm talking about. You drive a couple nails into wood already soft from what it's weathered, and everything looks fine at first. But after you pack up and head off, then what's to keep that wood from splintering?

BEAU: I don't leave a job half done.

DEX: You awful confident your work will last for a man builds things out of nothing more than wood.

BEAU: I tell you, Dex, you don't mind me saying so, you could learn a thing or two from wood. Something that bends lasts a whole lot longer than something stiff.

DEX: What makes you think you're building something meant to last? You talk like this is your own house to live in that you're fixing. A shed out back, that's all it is. That's all it's ever gonna be.

BEAU: I only know how to make things one way—as if they were my own.

DEX: All this, you fooling yourself you think it's any more than temporary. That shed out back, put up new walls, replace the roof, it still won't matter. The next strong wind that comes along will blow it down again.

BEAU: Long as I got my hammer and an apron full of nails, it won't stay down for long.

X: If that were really true, your own house would've been fit a while ago for you and the boy to move back in again.

BEAU: You're not talking some little shed without plumbing or electricity. You any idea what it would take to fix my house?

DEX: I didn't say it wouldn't be a job. Still, it's obvious your son's unhappy living here. You'd think a father would make a bigger effort to please his child.

BEAU: You would, wouldn't you? A father had a child unhappy with the life she led, you'd think her daddy would put aside his own feelings and let her have what happiness came her way.

DEX: You ain't never told your son "no" when it came to pleasure?

BEAU: There's a big difference between a boy of sixteen and a woman in her thirties.

DEX: Not when it comes to a father's love, there ain't.

BEAU: You think I'd hurt your daughter?

DEX: You think the world will give you any choice? You tell me some future where the two of you could ever be happy together.

BEAU: Things are changing, Dex. The flood washed away what used to be. Something new could take its place.

DEX: You really think that things are ever gonna change down here? They already going back to the way they always was— and worse.

BEAU: But look at us, you and me, black and white, living here together under one roof.

DEX: Yeah, with a wall running between us.

(*Lights fade.*)

(BEAU and MATTIE are drinking wine on the porch after dinner.)

MATTIE: That was some good, the meal you fixed. You don't
    watch out, you gonna have to give up carpentry and open a
    restaurant.

BEAU: Same thing, really. Carpentry and cooking, they both come
    down to measuring.

MATTIE: Measuring? So that's your secret?

BEAU: The secret to everything, you ask me. Measure twice, cut
    once. Save people a whole lot of grief, they followed that rule
    more often.

MATTIE: It's true. What use is a stick cut too short?

BEAU: You can make it work all right, you some one-tack carpenter
    too lazy to do the job right, but a board too short'll never hold
    the weight of something cut to fit.

MATTIE: So what about us, Beau? You and me, we cut to fit?

BEAU: I don't recall doing any measuring.

MATTIE: Since when you need a ruler? I seen you eye that pile of
    wood out back, working on the shed, and pick a scrap of two-
    by-four just the size you need.

BEAU: You know how carpenters entertain themselves at lunch?
    We sit in the shade and bet on lengths of wood. Somebody
    says, "That one-by-twelve beside the puddle looks like thirty-
    eight and a quarter inches long to me." Then somebody else
    goes, "You blind, old timer. I make that thirty-seven and five-

eighths, maximum." A third man, he thinks it's somewhere in between. Then we send an apprentice out to measure with a rule.

MATTIE: Anybody ever right?

BEAU: Somebody's always right, you bet that close. These aren't no amateurs we talking about. Journeyman and master carpenters, every one of them.

MATTIE: Right to an eighth of an inch?

BEAU: I don't know how we keep our balance neither, standing on a beam not four inches wide, driving nails into a rafter overhead. But ain't none of us ever fall.

MATTIE: Probably couldn't do it if you thought about it.

BEAU: Just like us. (*Pause.*) I let myself think about what we're doing, you and me, I'd wind up falling. Tell you, Mattie, feels like I'm St. Peter walking on the water or something, afraid to stop, afraid to look down for even half a second.

MATTIE: Afraid you'll remember you're nothing but a man, huh? (*Pause.*) You know, Beau, walking on water's not the only way to cross a river.

BEAU: But however you get there, once you reach the other side, sometimes there's no going back. (*Pause.*) To do what you want, I have to act like Audrey is just some kind of dream I got to wake up from.

MATTIE: Last thing I intend is take anybody's place. All I'm after, Beau, all I really want is just to have a man lets me be a woman now and then.

BEAU (*smiling*): And what are you the rest of the time you not some woman?

MATTIE: Same as you. Just somebody can't fall asleep, dragging herself through a city shattered into so many pieces, nobody's ever gonna put it back together again. (*Pause.*) But then, for a few hours, lying in your arms in the dark, I close my eyes, and you and me, it's just like they call it, we sleep together.

BEAU: Yeah, they named it right—though I never used to understand why they called it that.

(Pause.)

MATTIE: Daddy tells me the two of you had yourselves a little talk.

BEAU: Yeah, about the shed out back.

MATTIE: The shed, huh? 'Cause he gave me the impression you got into more than that.

BEAU: Well, yeah, eventually. He don't hold out much hope for the two of us.

MATTIE: It's hard for him to swallow, his daughter with a white man.

BEAU: My father were still alive, he'd throw a fit, too.

MATTIE: But how about you, Beau? What do you make of us, you with me?

BEAU: You know, all those years we were together, Audrey and me, if somebody would ask, "What color are your wife's eyes?" I'd always have to think about it for a second. Drove Audrey crazy, I couldn't remember. But that kind of thing, it's not what I see when I look at somebody I got feelings for.

MATTIE: It's not just the color of my eyes we talking about.

(Lights fade.)

(*In the middle of an argument, DEX pursues MATTIE through her front door onto the porch.*)

MATTIE: Just let me be.

DEX: Where you think all this is heading, what you doing?

MATTIE: You'd rather I live alone the rest of my life?

DEX: I'd rather you love somebody's not gonna break your heart before he's done.

MATTIE: Beau's not that kind of man.

DEX: You think it's always up to us how things turn out?

MATTIE: Oh, yeah, that's just like you, isn't it, Daddy? Not your fault, things fall apart.

DEX: You any different? Always blaming somebody else you all alone.

MATTIE: And what would you prefer I do? Look the other way like Mama did?

DEX: What went on between me and your mama, that ain't none of your business.

MATTIE: Now you live in my house, it is. Now you have me running day and night to serve you hand and foot like Mama did, it surely is my business how you act.

DEX: Don't you forget you're my daughter, girl.

MATTIE: And don't you forget you're a guest in my house.

DEX: Guest? That's all you think of me?

MATTIE: I think I ain't your little girl to boss around anymore. That's what I think.

DEX: You ungrateful child, you.

MATTIE: I deny you anything? You ask, there's something I don't do?

DEX: But you make me ask, Mattie. For every damn thing I need.

MATTIE: Well, how am I supposed to know what you need before you say?

DEX: Your mother never needed me to tell her.

MATTIE: I am not your wife.

DEX: And sounds to me you sorry to be my daughter.

(*Silence.*)

MATTIE: Daddy, I know you been through something awful.

DEX: Oh, what do you know, girl? You lose your house? You see your neighbor's body come floating by? You go and beg your own child for a place to sleep?

MATTIE: I never made you beg for nothing.

DEX: Oh, yeah? (*Imitating MATTIE.*) "You already run through all that money I just gave you, Daddy? And what's wrong with sleeping on a sofa, anyway. And no, you can't have the other side of my shotgun for yourself, old man. I need the rent to pay my mortgage."

MATTIE: I let you live next door, I lose this place. I offer you the bedroom, you won't take it. At work, I'm skipping lunches to give you spending money.

DEX: You any idea the way it makes me feel—no house, no job, nowhere but the armrest of a sofa to lay my head? My child going hungry so I got something in my pocket. You any idea the way it makes me feel, a man like me? I pay my way my whole damn life, and now I wind up living off my daughter.

MATTIE: It ain't your fault, Daddy. Some things, like you say, they can't be helped.

DEX: Just like you and your tenant, Mattie. Whole lot of suffering, all the good intentions in the world can't stop it happening.

MATTIE: Wouldn't be the first time my heart got broken.

DEX: You expect your father to stand around and let that happen?

MATTIE (*going back inside*): Like you say, Daddy, ain't always up to people how things turn out.

(*MATTIE exits, but DEX stays on the porch. BEAU and EUGENE enter their kitchen, arguing.*)

BEAU: And I say you're not.

EUGENE: You act like there's some reason for me to listen to you anymore.

BEAU: Keep it up, I'll give you a good goddamn reason to pay attention when I talk.

EUGENE: Yeah, go ahead and try.

(*Silence.*)

BEAU: What do you want me to say? That I'm the reason your mama died? (*Pause.*) All right. It wasn't for me, you'd still have a mother. You satisfied?

EUGENE: Well, at least now we agree on one thing.

BEAU: But you get older, Gene, this is all gonna look different to you. Way different.

EUGENE: That's your reason for everything, isn't it? I'm just too young to understand. I was older, I'd see right away you, you're innocent in all this.

BEAU: You burning up with anger, I know. But so am I. Only difference is, you got somebody to blame.

EUGENE: You looking for sympathy from me?

BEAU: Sympathy? I'm just saying I understand how angry you are.

EUGENE: Understand? You don't begin to understand. (*Pause.*) I put all this behind me like you want, then what happens to Mama? We dump her by the side of the road and move on?

BEAU: No, of course not. But eventually, babe, you got to lay her down somewhere. You can't go through life carrying her in your arms.

EUGENE: And who's gonna watch over her, I lay her down?

BEAU: Her husband.

EUGENE: You mean the husband's already got some other woman in his bed? That the grief-stricken husband you talking about?

BEAU: How many times you want to hear me say I'm guilty?

EUGENE: Every minute of every day for the rest of your life.

BEAU: You tell yourself this is all about your mama, but you stop to think what your mother would say, she were here? She be proud of you, she heard you talking to me like this?

EUGENE: You got no right bringing her up. Not after what you done . . . And you don't fool me. You just looking for forgiveness.

(*EUGENE exits.*)

BEAU (*to himself*): There's only one person could forgive me. (*Pause.*) And she's dead.

(*BEAU exits.*)

DEX (*to EUGENE as he storms out of his house with his book bag*): Pass by, you don't say hello to your old neighbor, son?

EUGENE (*turning to face DEX in surprise*): You talking to me?

DEX: We neighbors, ain't we?

EUGENE: Well, yeah, but you never so much as nod your head, I step on the porch.

DEX: So maybe it's time we get to know each other, you and me.

EUGENE: I got a lot of homework.

DEX: And all night to do it. (*Pause.*) So you like it any better'n I do, things going on around here?

EUGENE: You mean between my daddy and your daughter? (*Pause.*) What do you think?

DEX: Think if I was you, I'd be doing something about it.

EUGENE: Like what?

DEX: How's your house coming? I know I had enough of a house left to rebuild, I'd be over there night and day fixing it up to move back in.

EUGENE: If it were up to me, we'd be back home already. But my father says we can't live that way—you know, without gas and electricity.

DEX: You want to move back in your house so bad, then don't sit around here moping all the time. Go fix the place yourself, you want to live there.

EUGENE: But what about my father?

DEX: There some kind of law say you got to wait around for him?

EUGENE: But where am I supposed to get the money to fix things up?

DEX: What exactly you need to do?

EUGENE: Well . . . the city never turned the water off. The toilet still works—

DEX: So you got running water in the kitchen—and a shower. That's a start.

EUGENE: But without gas, there's no hot water in the place.

DEX: Cold showers'll make a man of you.

EUGENE: Got a room or two livable, Daddy and me could sleep there while we're working on the rest.

DEX: And what would that take?

EUGENE: First off, we got hundreds of nails still in the studs from where we ripped the sheetrock out. So pull all them. Then kill the mold and clean the place real good.

DEX: Shit, you ain't talking no money, boy. Let me see Willie can't come up with what you need. You do all that, how your father gonna say no to you about the rest?

EUGENE: That's some job, killing all the mold and cleaning up.

DEX: You want to whine like a tiny baby or you want to move back home again?

EUGENE: You really think I could do the work myself?

DEX: Boy, New Orleans ain't no place for little children no more.

EUGENE: Like you say, what choice would Daddy have, I got things started?

DEX: Now you talking like a man.

(*Lights fade.*)

SCENE 6

(*At night, BEAU enters his kitchen from the bedroom, followed by MATTIE.*)

MATTIE: Can't sleep again?

BEAU: Wish I could.

MATTIE: What's wrong, baby? Your boy's over at his friend's. We got the night to ourselves.

BEAU: No, we don't.

MATTIE: It's wrong to turn your wife into some kind of ghost won't let you sleep.

BEAU: It's not Audrey haunts me.

MATTIE: Then who?

BEAU: Me. What I done, I mean. What I didn't do. Me, I'm the one wandering around in the dark can't rest, not Audrey.

MATTIE: So you the one turned into a ghost?

BEAU: I told you already, wouldn't surprise me, somebody come up and say I'm dead and just don't know it.

MATTIE: I know that feeling, all right. Walking around like some kind of skeleton. (*Pause.*) But the truth is, I don't feel that way anymore, Beau. I see you coming down the street at night, all of a sudden, there's flesh on these bones, a heart beating in my chest.

BEAU: I'd be lying I said it wasn't the same for me.

MATTIE: And I can't go back to living the old way. Get up and go to work and come back home again to some empty house don't even know I'm there.

BEAU: But me, I can't go on living this new way, Mattie, you and me like we doing.

MATTIE: Why? I'm not asking you for anything.

BEAU: Who you think you fooling, woman? You asking me for everything. Every single thing I still got left.

MATTIE: You think I'm not offering the same in return?

BEAU: This all starts, it's just the one night. But now we talking something else entirely.

MATTIE: You strike a match, sometimes the house goes up in flames.

BEAU: That's the thing. It leaves you without a roof over your head, that happens.

MATTIE: We don't have a roof, I'll sleep under the stars with you, Beau.

BEAU: If only I could sleep.

MATTIE: Once you forget how, it takes time, learning to sleep again.

BEAU: But with all the time in the world, Mattie, your father ever gonna get used to the idea of you with me? (*Pause.*) And Eugene . . .

MATTIE: Eugene's starting to understand, isn't he?

BEAU: Understands the way he might come home the night of a funeral and find his daddy drunk at the kitchen table. Next day, though, he expects his father to wake up sober and go to work, no matter who got buried the day before.

MATTIE: And you and me, we don't have as much right as those depending on us?

BEAU: Not compared to a son needs his father, no.

MATTIE: You think I'm not depending on you, too? (*Pause.*) Or is it, you don't think we could make a go of it, a white man and a black woman, on either side the river?

BEAU: You notice anybody happy for us?

MATTIE: You keep talking everybody else. But you, Beau, what do you want?

BEAU: Me? I want to feel like I used to feel. Like I was living up to my obligations.

MATTIE: What about your obligations to the woman just was in
that bedroom with you?
BEAU: Think I even know who it is with me in there? I wake up in
the middle of the night, that woman lying there beside me in
the dark, think I remember it's you? I'm scared to death to fall
asleep for what it's like to wake up in that bed.

(*Lights fade.*)

(Morning. WILLIE sits on the porch steps. DEX enters from the street carrying a bag of doughnuts.)

DEX: Hey, man, what you doing over here on Sunday morning? How come you not still sleeping off Saturday night?

WILLIE: Didn't do nothing last night.

DEX: You getting old or something?

WILLIE: Maybe that's what's wrong with me. I don't know.

DEX (*wearily sitting down beside WILLIE*): Tell you, boy, I don't need no convincing that's what's wrong with me.

WILLIE: Naw, man, you look the same you always looked.

DEX (*pointing at WILLIE*): That's the first to go, you know, your memory.

WILLIE: Just saying, how you any different than you always been?

DEX: Me? (*Taking a doughnut from the bag.*) I'm like one of these doughnuts. Fine around the edges, but a hole shot through the middle of it.

(He takes a bite.)

WILLIE: What you talking about?

DEX: You ever see a man know what he was doing use a knife?

WILLIE: Knife? When anybody ever get killed with a knife anymore—except the middle of the night in the hands of some pissed-off woman, maybe?

DEX: Used to be a lot more popular, knives. Man knew how to use one, he'd never go straight for the heart.

WILLIE: No?

DEX: He'd catch you on the hand, slice your arm real bad, slash you good across the cheek. But take his time, let you bleed awhile before he'd move back in again.

WILLIE: Patient, huh?

DEX: Like he had the whole damn night and nothing else to do. Time he was done, you'd have so many cuts, couldn't tell just where the blood was coming from. Me, I used to think getting old was same as that. A hundred little nicks you hardly even notice till nothing's left of you but shreds.

WILLIE: Dex, you ain't old.

DEX: But it don't happen like that, little by little. (*He holds up another doughnut from the bag.*) Sudden as a bullet through your heart.

WILLIE (*taking the new doughnut from DEX and eating it*): So Father Time, he don't cut you down with that long-ass blade of his?

DEX: Hell no. That shriveled-up old white man, he's got himself a gun and knows how to use it.

WILLIE: Come on, man, you just tired is all.

DEX: Oh, I'm tired all right. Sleeping on my daughter's sofa, I'll never get a good night's rest again.

WILLIE: Yeah, lately I don't sleep so good myself.

(*Silence.*)

You ever think about the baby me and Mattie had?

DEX: Yolanda? Couldn't wait to come back home from work and play with her, that little girl. Swing her up and down and call her "Yo-Yo."

WILLIE: Don't know why, but she was on my mind last night.

DEX: The bad things, just the opposite from everything else. The older you get, the *more* you remember them.

WILLIE: Maybe I am getting old, then. (*Pause.*) Your daughter at church, I suppose.

DEX: Mmmhmm. And lucky for you. The girl's in quite a mood this morning.

WILLIE: Why's that?

DEX: Why you think?

WILLIE: Ain't going so good?

DEX: I keep telling her to stop this foolishness, but think she listens?

WILLIE: Don't have to tell me. She never seems to hear a word I say, neither.

DEX: You say what she wants to hear, she'll listen all right.

WILLIE: Well, I better figure out soon what that woman's waiting to hear.

(*He takes another doughnut from the bag in DEX's hand.*)

'Cause you ain't the only man in this town just the edges holding him together.

(*WILLIE is about to take a bite from the doughnut, but DEX snatches it away and takes a bite himself. Lights fade.*)

(*EUGENE, listening to music on headphones, is doing homework at the kitchen table. BEAU enters, coming home from his job. He motions for EUGENE to take off the headphones.*)

BEAU: I run by our house this afternoon on the way home. Guess what I see?

EUGENE: You tell me.

BEAU: Somebody's been working on the place.

EUGENE: Robbie and me, we been spending time over there.

BEAU: I was thinking maybe I could come give you a hand. After work, on weekends.

EUGENE: You sure Miss Godchaux can spare you?

BEAU: Boy, you ain't half as heartless as you pretend to be.

EUGENE: Yeah, that's true. When it comes to heartless, you got me beat.

(*Silence.*)

BEAU (*trying again*): Somebody actually knows what the hell he's doing might speed the job along.

EUGENE: If we could get just a room or two in livable condition, then you and me could stay there while we put the rest of the house back in shape.

BEAU: It didn't look like you're close to that just yet.

(*Silence.*)

EUGENE: It was Mr. Godchaux's idea, me fixing up the house myself.

BEAU: Dex?

EUGENE: Said, just go fix the house myself, I want to live there. Next day, me and Robbie, we got started.

BEAU: And Robbie comes gets you every day?

EUGENE: Yeah, we split the tolls. One day we work on our house, next day we work on his. That's why we weren't there tonight when you came by. Over at his place, bleaching off the mold.

BEAU: That's some job.

EUGENE: Mr. Godchaux says it's time we all grew up. This ain't no place for little children now, he says.

BEAU: But what you planning on doing about your school, we move back home?

EUGENE: I already checked on that. We move back in, I can go to any school that's open. Even Robbie's school, I want. He said he'll pick me up and take me home again, I sign up there.

BEAU: You really thought this through, I see.

EUGENE: So how long it's gonna take to get it to the point where we can live there?

BEAU: The house? I don't know. It's getting warmer now, so we won't freeze there anymore. We'd need to finish killing off the mold before we moved back in.

EUGENE: But just to get a room or two together where we could live?

BEAU: If I could get my hands on some insulation and some sheetrock—

EUGENE: Mr. Godchaux says Willie'll get us anything we need. And cheap, he says.

BEAU: I'll bet it's cheap. (*Pause.*) But let's say he can get us some. We first find ourselves an electrician to rewire the two back rooms. Then a day or so to set the insulation and float the rock. Maybe a weekend to do something with the floor—bleach it, clean it somehow—and hang the millwork.

EUGENE: So just a week or two?

BEAU: I'll get a plumber off my job to check out all the plumbing in the house. Add another weekend for that and everything else we haven't thought about.

EUGENE: So end of the month?

BEAU: Nothing fancy, now. Just sheetrock and a concrete floor.

EUGENE: So we gonna move back in?

BEAU: I guess it's like Dex says: Time we all grow up and do our jobs.

(*Lights fade.*)

SCENE 9

*(Late morning on the front porch of the shotgun. EUGENE
carries out a box of household goods and clothing. BEAU follows
with his guitar. WILLIE enters.)*

WILLIE: Dex said y'all moving, huh?

EUGENE: Back home.

(EUGENE, smiling, carries his box offstage to their truck.)

WILLIE: So that insulation and sheetrock work out all right?

BEAU: Yeah, appreciate it, what you done. Finished two bedrooms
with it.

WILLIE: Afraid you'll have to look someplace else, though, you
want any more.

BEAU (*putting down his guitar*): How come? That was quality rock
you got me—and cheap.

WILLIE: Started a business of my own.

BEAU: What's that?

WILLIE: Grass cutting. (*He hands BEAU a business card.*) All the
abandoned houses, people gonna need somebody to hack
down the weeds, now that winter's over.

BEAU: The place is so overgrown, the city's turning back into a
swamp.

WILLIE: I got me a mower and this little trailer.

BEAU: Wondered why I hadn't seen you 'round here lately. Tell you, you gonna make yourself some money with a business like that in this godforsaken city.

WILLIE: Yeah, maybe eventually hire me a crew, expand to more neighborhoods, like where you and the boy are headed. Anybody else on your block move back yet?

BEAU: No, we're the only ones. Got a family in a trailer on the next block, though. And people across the street say they coming back this summer.

WILLIE: Shit, I wouldn't want to be out there all by my lonesome. No grocery stores, no service stations, no nothing.

BEAU: No, just me and Gene and rats the size of cats. But they got soldiers in Humvees cruise around at night.

WILLIE: Well, listen, you be careful.

BEAU: You, too, Willie.

WILLIE: It's Clarence, man.

BEAU: Clarence? (*Pause.*) Well, Clarence, you watch yourself, too.

(*MATTIE steps onto the porch and watches as they shake hands. EUGENE returns and goes inside to get another box.*)

WILLIE (*to MATTIE*): I come by to see if maybe you need your grass cut.

MATTIE: That's sweet, Clarence, but—

WILLIE: I'll swing back a little later with my mower.

MATTIE: We'll see.

WILLIE (*handing MATTIE his business card*): No, you gonna see.

(*WILLIE exits.*)

BEAU (*as EUGENE comes out with another box*): Much more left inside?

EUGENE: This is it.

BEAU: Well, you go tie a tarp over the things in the back of the truck in case it rains. But let me have your house key first.

(*EUGENE exits to the truck offstage.*)

MATTIE: So you all ready to go, huh?

BEAU: Just about. Wanted to give you our keys before we left.

MATTIE: Let me go and get my checkbook. I'll give you back the deposit that you paid.

BEAU: Yeah, you can't send it to us. Half a year and more since the water went down, and still they say they can't deliver mail to streets that flooded.

MATTIE: Hang on. I'll be right back.

(*MATTIE exits, then DEX comes out onto the porch.*)

DEX: So now you on your way, huh, back to your own house?

BEAU: Yeah, just the way you wanted it, I guess.

DEX: You doing the right thing, especially for the boy.

BEAU: You didn't leave me much choice, did you? Goading the boy into shaming me about the house. What was I gonna do after he did all that work but finish it?

DEX: Now don't go blaming me. Sooner or later, you had to fix your house and move back home. I told you this would never last.

BEAU: But what am I going back home to?

DEX: At least you got a home. Me, I'll be sleeping on that miserable couch of hers the rest of my life.

BEAU: You mean to say you not moving in the vacant side this afternoon?

DEX: Not without the rent to pay my daughter's mortgage, no.

BEAU: So you got your way on everything else but what you really wanted.

DEX: Think it don't break my heart, what happened to you? I know damn well what it's like to lose a wife you love.

(*MATTIE returns.*)

I'll go give your boy a hand.

(DEX exits to the truck offstage.)

MATTIE: So here's your check.

BEAU: We ought to talk before I go.

MATTIE: What's left for us to say? Everybody tells me you have to go. (*Pause.*) But we could've made it, Beau, you and me.

BEAU: With everyone against us? Your father, my son, and everybody else?

MATTIE: Everybody else, that's just excuses. It's only what's inside your own heart that matters.

BEAU: You think that wasn't set against us, too? Or set against itself, at least? My wife dead not five months, and I start up with you.

MATTIE: This was a normal world, we'd 've known what to do. But call this normal, how we living now? I don't know a set of rules exists for life in a place like this.

BEAU: I'm walking away with no regret for anything that happened here.

MATTIE: But why you walking away at all?

BEAU: Because even after everything we done, I'm still father to a son and husband to another woman. (*Pause.*) You never noticed, not in all the time we been together, you never noticed this wedding ring I wear?

MATTIE: You think there was a single night I ever forgot it was wrapped around your finger?

BEAU: I just don't know how to stop being who I've always been, Mattie.

(BEAU steps toward her, but she holds up her hand to stop him, perhaps pressing the deposit check against his chest. Fighting back tears, she goes inside.)

DEX (*coming back from the truck offstage, having witnessed the last exchange*): So you finish up what you started here?

BEAU: What?

DEX: You know, the shed out back you started fixing.

BEAU: Yeah, it's all done. Like nothing ever happened here.

DEX: Don't you believe that, Beau. Better or worse, there's nothing the same as what it was before the flood.

BEAU: Nothing I can think of came out better than before.

DEX: Yeah, it's true, the city, it's all turning out worse than anybody could've ever dreamed. But your boy, Eugene, you must be proud of him for what he's done. And you, even with all you lost, you going back to your own home again.

BEAU: Just the way you wanted it.

DEX: All I ever wanted, Beau, was make my daughter happy.

BEAU: You go inside, you'll find her crying there.

DEX: That wasn't me made her cry.

BEAU: So you knew from the beginning I'd leave her in tears, huh?

DEX: All this old man knew from the beginning, boy, you looking for a happy ending in this world, go buy yourself a book. (*Pause.*) You take care of yourself, Beau, and that child of yours.

BEAU: Yeah, and you take care of that child of yours, Dex.

(*BEAU starts to exit.*)

DEX (*noticing BEAU's guitar on the porch*): Hey, man, you forgetting your guitar.

BEAU (*turning back, then stopping*): Tell you what, why don't you hang on to it? Last thing my boy needs is listen to his daddy singing sad songs all night.

DEX: I already told you, Beau, what you do, ain't nobody would call that singing.

(*BEAU smiles and holds up his hand in farewell before exiting. DEX sits down wearily on the steps, strums the guitar a few times, and then starts singing.*)

Sometimes I live in the country,
And sometimes I live in town,
And sometimes I take a great notion
To jump into the river and drown.

(*As the music continues, MATTIE comes back out onto the porch and hangs the "For Rent" sign on the front door of the shotgun's vacant side. She turns and looks in the direction BEAU has exited. DEX keeps his eyes on his daughter. Fade to blackout.*)

MOLD

———— ×✗× ————

Mold premiered at Southern Rep Theatre, Aimée Hayes, Producing Artistic Director, in New Orleans on March 20, 2013. It was directed by Mark Routhier with the following cast:

EMILE "TREY" GUIDRY............................ Trey Burvant

MARIE GUIDRY.. Kerry Cahill

AMELIA DELACHAISE............................. Carol Sutton

EDGAR BERNARD............................. Randy Maggiore

Scenic design by Geoffrey Hall
Lighting design by Marty Sachs
Costumes by Veronica Russell
Sound design by Mike Harkins
Production Stage Manager: Liz Harwood

ACT I

(Lights up on the porch of a house flooded in the levee collapse a year earlier. A brown waterline higher than the front door stains the wall. A rusted porch chair lies on its side; another is still upright. Behind a rusted screen door, perhaps wedged open, a large red "X" is spray painted on the front door with "9–21" at the top quadrant of the X, "0" on the right, "CA7" on the left, and "2 dead" at the bottom; it can be seen only when the door is open. In darkness behind the front door is the living room of the ruined house. Having been untouched since flooding, it is still in shambles with mold scrawling over the walls and the furniture, including a sofa and scattered chairs. Scales of gray mud glaze most surfaces. Mounds of moldering clothes, broken lamps, a television set, and other trash cover the buckled floor. Everything is askew from having floated around the room. A portrait of the Sacred Heart or, perhaps, Our Lady of Perpetual Help still hangs on the wall, covered with mold. Overhead, the moldy blades of a fan droop like the petals of a wilted flower. Water-stained, moldy curtains cover any windows. An interior hallway leads away from the living room; folding attic stairs, still down, can be glimpsed in the hall. Carrying a cooler of beer and bottled water, TREY and MARIE approach the porch.)

TREY: My God, look at this place.
MARIE: The grass . . . What kind of grass is this, it gets so high?

(Silence.)

159

MARIE: Looks like somebody dropped a bomb here.
TREY: Like there's been a war.
MARIE: Yeah, and we lost.

(*Silence.*)

TREY: Everything's so gray.
MARIE: The saltwater leached out all the color, I guess.

(*Pause.*)

But look, your mama's roses, they still alive. Some of them anyway. And that was her scrawniest bush, that bush there. Now look at it.

(*Pause.*)

Her camellias, though, not a one made it. Hard to tell what's gonna thrive and what's gonna wither, you go through something like this.

(*Silence. MARIE touches TREY, but he twists away slightly.*)

TREY: Mr. Joe's truck across the street. Look at that.
MARIE: How'd it get that way? How's that possible?
TREY: Floated up on top of there, I guess.
MARIE: They just leave it like that for a whole year?
TREY: Everything's somewhere it's not supposed to be.

(*Pause.*)

MARIE: Which direction was that little grocery made the Italian sausage your daddy liked so much?
TREY (*pointing*): Over there—no, that way.

(*Pause.*)

It does take a minute to get your bearings.

MARIE (*stepping onto the porch*): Well, you ready?

TREY (*hanging back*): Maybe we ought to wait for the insurance adjustor before we unlock the place. Let him see we didn't change the way it looks inside.

MARIE: We don't have to go in yet, baby. We're early.

TREY: No, it's just . . .

MARIE: Why don't we sit out here a while?

TREY (*righting the porch chair on its side and offering it to MARIE*): Yeah, let's sit a minute. You don't look so good.

MARIE (*sitting*): No, I'm all right. Just hot is all.

TREY (*sitting in the other chair or on the cooler*): I don't feel so good myself. Maybe we both coming down with something.

(*Silence.*)

MARIE: It's hard. Being back here.

TREY: That was some long drive.

MARIE: It's always longer than you think it's gonna be coming over here.

TREY: 'Cause Houston looks so close on the map.

(*Pause.*)

MARIE: Good we left while it was dark and still a little cool.

TREY: Yeah, once the sun come up, that damn glare off the hood like to blind me.

MARIE: And driving west, we'll have it back in our eyes going home if we don't leave as soon as we're done with the adjustor.

TREY: Don't worry. I'm not looking to stay here any longer than it takes to settle up about the insurance money. Like you been saying, there's nothing to keep us in New Orleans anymore.

MARIE: And I've got to be at work early tomorrow.

TREY: They call a meeting every Monday morning, don't they?

MARIE: It's the new manager. But what good all these meetings do, I don't know. Same number of customers come through my check-out now as when Mr. Healey ran the store. And he never pays attention to a thing I say.

TREY: Well, maybe they'll promote this new guy on out of there and make you the next manager.

MARIE: The other girls tell me they've never once had a woman run the store.

TREY: Afraid she'll get pregnant on them and quit, I guess.

MARIE: Yeah, I'm sure that's the reason, Trey.

TREY: I'm not saying I agree with them.

(*Opening the ice chest.*)

You want a beer, Marie?

MARIE: No, let me have a bottle of that water. Maybe it'll calm my stomach.

(*TREY hands her a water bottle and opens a beer for himself.*)

You start in drinking beer this early in the day, you better hope the toilet still works.

TREY: I'll go behind the house, I have to. Ain't nobody out here to see but you.

MARIE: It's like everybody's just given up on the neighborhood.

(*Pause.*)

TREY: I was a boy, we'd sit out here till dark listening to the cicadas up in the trees. Now they got brown widow spiders instead.

MARIE: They poisonous?

TREY: Won't kill you, just paralyze your arm or leg for a little while.

MARIE: Where they come from?

TREY: Floated in on the flood, I guess. Like these big lizards they got here now killing off the little green ones. Used to let them bite our earlobes, and we'd wear them like earrings. The green ones. Freaked Mama out, I walked in the house with two lizards hanging from my ears.

MARIE: Yeah, I wouldn't want my children wearing reptiles for jewelry, neither.

TREY: Speaking of which, you be careful in the yard, especially with the grass this high. God knows how many snakes swum in from the swamps. Always got water moccasins everywhere after a storm.

MARIE: But they strike slow, don't they? Not like the rattlers back home.

TREY: You step on one, you'll find out they fast enough. And the nearest emergency room left is way over in Jefferson Parish.

MARIE: You been keeping tabs on the city, huh?

TREY: Now and then, that's all.

MARIE: We do like we agreed—take the insurance money and put it down on a little place of our own over in Houston—we can make ourselves a new life.

TREY: No, you're right. It's just . . .

MARIE: Why don't we go in before the adjustor gets here? (*Pause.*) Honey, you don't want to walk through the house for the first time with some stranger standing there next to you.

TREY: Yeah, maybe we ought to take a look. See what to talk to the adjustor about.

MARIE: You got the key?

TREY (*checking his pockets*): I thought you had it.

MARIE: I left it on the table so you wouldn't forget it again the way you did when we come for the funeral.

TREY: I must not've seen it there.

MARIE: It's still sitting on the kitchen table back in Houston?

TREY (*starting to exit*): I'll go around back, see if I can't find a way in.

MARIE: Hang on, Trey. You try the knob yet?

TREY: You know that door's never unlocked.
MARIE: Yeah, but the soldiers might have opened it from the inside.

(*She tries the door, which is unlocked.*)

The knob turns, but the door still won't open.
TREY (*returning to the porch*): Let me try.

(*He shoulders the door open. Lights up on the living room.*)

My God.

(*They enter and wander around the room.*)

The smell. I never smelled anything like this.
MARIE (*almost in tears*): How did the sofa get all the way over here?
TREY: Ain't nothing where it used to be.
MARIE: No, it's all every which way, the room.
TREY: Watch where you step, Marie, you don't get cut on
    something broken.
MARIE: Who'd ever guess water could do this to a house?
TREY: Nobody could imagine it, what went on here.
MARIE: It leaves you dizzy, don't it, the house like this?
TREY: It's an oven in here.
MARIE: I'm getting sick. I need some air.

(*She returns to the porch and leans over the railing. TREY
remains in the house until he looks down the hallway and sees
the attic stairs still down. He follows them up to the attic with
his eyes, then makes his way to MARIE on the porch.*)

TREY: You OK?
MARIE: Yeah, just the smell and the heat and all.
TREY: You see the pictures on the TV, but you don't know what it's
    gonna be like, you open the door.

MARIE: How could you know what to expect? How could anybody, unless they've been through it before? And who's ever been through this?

(*Pause.*)

TREY: I can't believe it's August again. A year, already, since the flood.

MARIE: Looks like a hundred years, don't it? Like we uncovered some old house been buried for a century.

TREY: Guess we should've done something about the place before now.

MARIE: I know this ain't easy for you, baby.

TREY: But we could've done something.

MARIE (*laughing tenderly*): Twice we come back to New Orleans, twice you forget the key. I should've stuck that key in my own pocket.

(*Pause.*)

TREY: The attic stairs are still down in the hallway.

(*Silence.*)

MARIE: Let's go look, see we can't find some keepsakes inside we can bring home to Texas. Before the adjustor gets here, I mean.

TREY (*hesitating, then nodding*): Yeah, let's go see there's anything worth keeping.

(*They enter the house and exit down the interior hallway.*)

(*Wearing an identification badge and carrying a clipboard, AMELIA enters, checks a form and knocks on the front door.*)

AMELIA: Yoohoo, anybody home?

(*AMELIA enters the house.*)

TREY (*returning from the hallway*): Help you?

AMELIA: Oh, you frightened me. I didn't know anybody was in here.

TREY: With the front door open?

AMELIA: Most the houses out here got their doors left wide open all the time.

MARIE (*entering from the hallway*): Hi, I'm Marie Guidry, and this is my husband, Trey. We've been expecting you.

AMELIA: Expecting me?

TREY: Well, not for another half hour or so.

AMELIA: I don't think I understand.

MARIE: You're the adjustor, aren't you?

AMELIA: Adjustor?

TREY: From the insurance company. We supposed to meet you here this morning.

AMELIA: Insurance company? Them thieves. Not me.

TREY: Well, who are you then?

AMELIA: Why, I'm Amelia. Mrs. Amelia Delachaise.

TREY: But what are you doing here, Mrs. Delachaise?

AMELIA (*showing them the identification badge she's wearing*): I work for the city. The Office of Code Enforcement.

TREY: Code Enforcement? What code?

AMELIA: You know, blighted properties.

MARIE: City Hall hired you, and you work on a Sunday?

AMELIA: Well, technically I'm a volunteer inspector.

TREY: But inspector of what?

AMELIA: You haven't heard about all this? The city sent the letters out, I don't know, months ago.

MARIE: I don't think the post office has delivered any mail out here since the flood.

AMELIA: Well, there was something on Channel 4 about it, too.

MARIE: They don't carry Channel 4 back home in Texas where we're living now.

TREY: But what's all this about some inspection you here for?

AMELIA: It's the Mayor's Good Neighbor Plan. I got a fact sheet right here they gave all the volunteers. They said the mayor came up with his plan to . . . wait a minute, it's on here somewhere. Yeah . . .

(Reading from the sheet.)

" . . . to protect citizens' properties and to implement safeguards to ensure that the financial investments of returning citizens are not depreciated by the intentional or unintentional failure of their neighbors to comply with the City ordinances."

MARIE: What's all that supposed to mean?

AMELIA: Wait, I got another copy in here somewhere. *(Rooting in her bag.)* Here you go, darlin.' Look there on page two. No, page two. Yeah, right there.

(Reading again.)

"City Ordinance № 22203 M.S.C., Section 26–262 (C) provides that every owner of a dwelling or dwelling unit shall take appropriate measures to complete the remediation of their properties, as soon as possible, but no later than August 29, 2006."

TREY: But that's the day after tomorrow.

AMELIA: Y'all really haven't heard about all this? I can't believe it. Look right there on that sheet your wife's got.

(Reading again.)

"The City of New Orleans Good Neighbor Plan is a proactive measure to educate its citizens on the options that property owners may exercise to comply with the Gutting Ordinance. The three options are as follows: (1) The property owner may gut, remediate and board; (2) The property owner may renovate or rebuild; and/or (3) The property owner may elect voluntary demolition."

TREY: Demolition? Hold on now. You saying we got until Tuesday to fix all this up, or else you gonna knock down the house?

MARIE: Voluntary demolition, Trey. Voluntary. We got options here.

AMELIA: This is the part where I come in.

(*Reading again.*)

"The Mayor's Office, Good Neighborhood Plan Task Force and neighborhood volunteers"—that's me—"will walk their neighborhoods to identify properties that are not in compliance with the City's Ordinance. The volunteers and city staff will have the ability to post courtesy notices on properties that are in violation of the City's Ordinance and subject to sanctions and/or liens, pursuant to the Public Nuisance laws."

TREY: So let me get this straight. You going around choosing which houses the city's gonna bulldoze?

AMELIA: Somebody's got to.

MARIE: And what about this house?

AMELIA: Well, you clearly in violation of the Gutting Ordinance. I got to cite you for that. And you got other issues. That grass out front—

TREY: We like our grass high.

AMELIA: Yeah, well, I got another sheet here talks about that, too.

(*Handing a copy to MARIE and then reading.*)

"Today, the City of New Orleans will launch the Imminent Health Threat Demolition Resident Assistance Program to educate property owners on the process and criteria to remove a property from the Imminent Health Threat demolition list."

TREY: Demolition list? Wait a minute, lady. You got us on some list already?

AMELIA (*holding up her hand in explanation as she continues to read*): "Property Removal Criteria: Property owners must provide proof and documentation, in mail or in person, that shows the following: (1) The property has been gutted and contents have been removed."

(*Looking around the room and shaking her head.*)

Unh-uh. "(2) Grass is cut in the front, back, side yards."

(*As if looking out a window at the yard.*)

Nope. "And (3) All doors closed and secured."

(*Shaking her head.*)

I don't think so.

(*Looking up from her clipboard.*)

It looks to me you in violation of all three.

MARIE: So you plan to tear this house down?

AMELIA: Oh, no, darlin.' (*She holds up an orange sheet of paper with "DEMOLITION NOTICE" printed in large letters across the top with fine print below.*) All I do is just tape this courtesy notice to the front door saying the city's gonna come demolish this place, that's all. (*She tapes the notice to the front door.*) And turn in the address on Monday morning to the volunteer coordinator.

TREY: Courtesy notice? That your idea of courtesy?

AMELIA: You rather the city knock down your house without any warning? Think that's more polite?

TREY: You mean to say you walk down the street and decide, "Let's tear down that home and that one and the other one"? That's how you spend your Sunday mornings?

AMELIA: You can't expect your neighbors to put up with a place looks like this.

TREY: What neighbors? There's not another human being for blocks.

AMELIA: And why you think that is? Think people want to move back next door to a house the weeds are three feet high?

TREY: We supposed to come mow our lawn in the middle of this wilderness?

AMELIA: That's the law, yeah.

TREY: How we supposed to do that living all the way over in Texas?

AMELIA: A whole year go by, and you can't find a weekend to come cut your grass? Please.

TREY: You gonna tear this house down because the lawn ain't mowed?

AMELIA: I didn't say that, sir. I said you got to remediate. That's all I said.

MARIE: So if we do what it says here—

TREY: But I don't "remediate," you gonna call in the bulldozers.

AMELIA: You want to scream and holler at me 'cause you ain't cut your grass in a year?

TREY: You gonna knock my house down.

AMELIA: Not me, sir, no. The city. The city's gonna knock it down. Unless you get busy and do something about it by the deadline.

TREY: You talking Tuesday I got to have this place remediated. That's crazy, what you saying.

AMELIA: That's the law, what I'm saying.

MARIE: They enforce that law, Mrs. Delachaise, there won't be a house left standing around here.

AMELIA: Yeah, darlin,' people tell me that, but it's mostly in neighborhoods they're over the fifty percent.

MARIE: Fifty percent?

AMELIA: I can't believe y'all haven't heard about all this.

TREY: You worrying about front lawns in a city the whole damn place is in ruins.

AMELIA: But that's just what I'm talking about. Remediating the ruins. (*Tapping her clipboard.*) It says right here if a residential structure is more than fifty percent damaged, FEMA is going to demolish it—but at taxpayer expense. It won't cost you a penny, as long as we get you over the fifty percent hurdle.

TREY: This house ain't fifty percent damaged.

AMELIA: Yeah, that's what they tried to pull on me, too. Said my place was only forty-seven percent. That's how I got involved with all this. Proving to the city my house was over fifty percent gone.

MARIE: They knocked down your house?

AMELIA: And it didn't cost me one red cent.

TREY: But this house—

AMELIA: Oh, don't you worry. It won't be a problem qualifying, not over here in this zip code. This neighborhood, I just turn in the address, they won't blink at fifty-five, sixty percent. Hell, I take a picture out front, as bad as it looks, they might go seventy percent—not that you need it that high.

MARIE: So if you put this notice on us, they'll come demolish the house for free?

TREY: But we gonna fix the place up. The only reason we over here this morning, come make some plans for putting things back in order.

AMELIA: I thought you said you over here to meet some insurance adjustor.

TREY: Yeah, to get the money to rebuild. Ain't that right, Marie?

MARIE: But, Trey—

TREY: We gonna put things back the way they used to be.

MARIE: Trey—

TREY: So we ain't sitting still for you waltzing in here and telling us you're tearing down the house. This house, it's got plenty of life left. Plenty.

AMELIA: And you had plenty of time to fix this house up before the city had to step in. It's for nothing but your neighbors' sake, this program we got.

TREY: Neighbors? Why don't you go stick those demolition signs of yours on the neighbors' houses before you come round here. They all falling down on themselves, anyway, those houses down the block.

AMELIA: Look, mister, I'm not the one spent the last year in Texas instead of seeing to his property. I mean, look at this place.

TREY: How's it any of your goddamn business what I choose to do?

AMELIA: You need to watch your mouth, sir.

TREY: Watch my mouth? You show up with your fuckin' courtesy notices and threaten me you gonna bulldoze this house.

AMELIA: I don't have to put up with your abuse, sir. You don't have no right—

TREY: Right? What right you got to come in here and threaten me.

AMELIA: Threaten you? You the one raising your voice, not me. And I don't appreciate it, not one little bit.

TREY: Who the fuck you think you are?

AMELIA: I work for the city.

TREY: Work? You nothing but a goddamn volunteer.

AMELIA (*reaching for her cell phone*): You keep it up, mister. Keep it up I'm calling nine-one-one, and I'm gonna get the police over here for your ass.

(*TREY advances toward AMELIA, who holds up her phone to his face as she presses the first number.*)

Nine.

MARIE: Trey, honey . . .

AMELIA (*still holding up her phone*): One.

MARIE: Trey.

AMELIA (*as she exits onto the porch and puts the phone to her ear*): One.

MARIE (*waving TREY away as she pursues AMELIA onto the porch*):
Why don't we talk, just the two of us, Mrs. Delachaise?

TREY (*shouting after AMELIA*): You think I'm letting the city knock
down my home, you out of your fuckin' mind, woman.

MARIE: Please, Mrs. Delachaise.

AMELIA (*putting down her phone*): You just lucky nobody
answered.

(*MARIE stands on the porch with AMELIA as TREY calms down
inside. As the conversation continues on the porch, TREY paces
and then disappears down the hallway*)

MARIE: I'm sorry about that, Mrs. Delachaise. My husband's
having a hard time with all this.

AMELIA: That don't give the man the right to holler at me like that.

MARIE: No, ma'am, absolutely not. But he's dealing with a lot, Trey.

AMELIA: Why would he talk that way to me? Use language like that.

MARIE: Once the insurance money comes in, we plan to sell this
house for whatever we can get and buy something permanent
in Houston.

AMELIA: And what's any of that got to do with me?

MARIE: Well, you show up and tell him the city's gonna come
demolish the place before we can sell it.

AMELIA: I'm just doing my job. It's not my fault what the law says.

MARIE: Yes, ma'am. It wasn't really you he was yelling at. He's just
so angry.

AMELIA: Well, hell, I get angry, too.

MARIE: There's no excuse, talking to you like that. You were just
doing your job.

AMELIA: That's right. And maybe I am just a volunteer, but
somebody's got to do something about the way this city looks.

MARIE: It can't go on like it is, everything in ruins.

AMELIA: Henry, my own husband, never spoke to me that way.
And your husband thinks he can say them kind of things to me?

MARIE: You just took him by surprise is all. We thought you were
the adjustor here to give us our money, and then you start
talking about remediation and demolition—
AMELIA: Adjustor? You don't want to know what I think of
insurance adjustors. They come through our neighborhood,
offer us half what they giving people live just a few blocks away.
MARIE: For the same kind of houses?
AMELIA: Same square footage. Built the same time as mine. Can't
tell no difference between them from the street.
MARIE: But they must've had some reason, no?
AMELIA: Oh, they had a reason all right. My neighbors, they all
black folks. You get over a few blocks, though, it turns lily
white in a hurry.
MARIE: But how'd they get away with that?
AMELIA: Girl, the way it is around here right now, people getting
away with whatever they want.
MARIE: Well, that's not right. You ought to do something about that.
AMELIA: And what are we supposed to do? Go hire us a lawyer
to take on the hundred lawyers the insurance company got
working for them? Shit.
MARIE: Still . . .
AMELIA: And how we gonna pay for even one lawyer? Ain't none
of us have any money left after everything we done lost.
MARIE: God, what people been through.
AMELIA (*sighing*): Yeah, your husband, too, I guess.
MARIE: You care for something to drink, Mrs. Delachaise?
AMELIA: That would be nice.

(*MARIE offers her a choice of a beer or a bottle of water from the
cooler. AMELIA points to the beer.*)

I'll take that one, baby.

(*MARIE puts the water away and opens a beer for AMELIA and
one for herself.*)

AMELIA (*sitting*): And truth be told, he ain't the first one to yell at me neither.

MARIE: I'm sorry, though. He had no right to talk to you like that.

AMELIA: Everybody's at the end of their rope by now.

MARIE (*taking a seat*): I've been dreading this trip, him being here again. Right after the flood, Trey comes up with this idea he's gonna rebuild the place and we're gonna move back here. But I talked him out of that foolishness.

AMELIA: You know, that was my first thought, too. Move back home. At least sitting in that shelter in Baton Rouge, that's what I was thinking. But then I saw what was left of my little place when I finally come back here. And that was end of that idea, living there again.

MARIE: Been there long?

AMELIA: Child, my whole married life. The cutest place you ever seen, and always clean as a whistle and neat as a pin—at least since Henry passed away. I stopped the *Picayune* the day we buried him. The ink comes off on everything you leave them on, the papers. I'm telling you, you let a newspaper in the house, you wind up with smudges everywhere. So that was the end of the *Picayune*, the day I come home from the graveyard.

MARIE: You stay through the storm?

AMELIA: Henry and me, we never once evacuated for a hurricane in all the years we were together, so why start now, I thought. Especially being alone and all, a widow like me. Where'd I go, for one thing? And who'd take care of my house, I did? You don't know what it was like after Betsy, when I was just a girl.

(*MARIE shakes her head.*)

No, you way too young for Betsy, huh? The looters everywhere, I mean, and what went on.

MARIE: It must've been frightening, though, riding out Katrina by yourself?

AMELIA: Not really. The storm, it comes and goes, just like they always do. I tell you, darlin,' I'm sitting on my sofa. The rain is done. The sky is turning blue. They had the power on, why, I could brew a pot of tea and serve it in the teacups that I got in Washington the time we went. The ones with all the presidents around the edge.

MARIE: Yeah, Trey's mama got spoons like that. Bet they still sitting in the kitchen drawer. She told me she used to feed him baby food with them when he was small.

AMELIA: The little ones, yeah. I used to see them for sale all the time in that magazine in the Sunday paper—at least until I cancel my subscription once Henry dies. They would have gone real nice with the teacups I had, those little spoons with the presidents engraved on them.

MARIE: Or maybe it was the states on them, not the presidents. I don't know.

AMELIA: I think you right. It was the states. But still, they would've gone OK with the cups I got. They go together, don't they? The presidents with the states, I mean. Anyway, like I say, I'm sitting there on my sofa just like us sitting here. One minute, my carpet's dry. Next thing I know, it's turning dark along the walls. I get up to see what's going on, and suddenly my carpet's soggy as my front lawn. And just that quick it's up around my ankles, the water rushing in my house. It takes a minute to realize what's happening when something happens you not expecting. And water coming underneath my door and through my walls, I'm not expecting that. Not with the storm long gone and me sitting on my sofa like I was. The flood's coming up so fast, girl, it don't leave me time to think. I open the front door, but the water rushes in so hard, I can't get out. So I grab a chair and stand on it. It's like that song they used to have, though, about the snake swallowing you little by little. You know, it swallows your feet, and then it swallows your knees, and then it swallows your hips—and just inches up the rest of you until it's right up to your throat.

MARIE: What did you do then?

AMELIA (*laughing*): Child, you just lift your chin, and you hold your breath.

MARIE: In some places, I heard it came up eight feet in ten minutes, the water.

(*Inside the house, TREY returns from the hallway with a flood-damaged photo album and pages through it.*)

AMELIA: Can you imagine that? You sitting on your sofa, thinking if the power is on, I'll make some tea. And not ten minutes later, you standing on a chair with water up around your mouth from God knows where. I tell you, darlin,' by then I'm praying to St. Jude because Danny Thomas—remember him, the comedian?—he used to raise money on the TV for those poor little children, the ones all sick and dying at the hospital named for him. Not for Danny Thomas. For St. Jude, I mean, since he's the patron saint of desperate situations. And standing on that little chair, the water in my living room just two feet from the ceiling now, I think I qualify to pray to him.

MARIE: Yes, ma'am. I think everybody down here qualifies to pray to the saint in charge of hopeless causes.

AMELIA: Well, I guess it works, because the flood slows down and stops right there, right under my chin. And that's when it all begins, the waiting for some help to come. But help don't come too soon, as it turns out. You ain't never seen nothing like what's going on inside my little house: the sofa floating 'round the living room until it starts to sink—just like the Titanic going down or something. You know, that was some movie, wasn't it? Henry wouldn't go, so I went with my sister, Imogene. Hates her name, my sister, so we call her Jeanie. I didn't agree with all the nudity, though. I mean, that girl has a pretty face. What does she need to go and show the rest of herself for?

MARIE: That naked girl's the only thing got Trey to watch it with me.

AMELIA (*laughing with MARIE*): Made me sad, too, the end, that boy dying. And it was just like that in my living room. The sofa disappearing under the water. Me all alone afraid to move for fear I'd drown. All sorts of things are bobbing past my eyes, things I haven't really noticed since we got them. Knickknacks and souvenirs and old-time bottles we found under my mama's house the Sunday when the pipes all froze twenty years ago. It makes you think, the water everywhere, all sorts of things. How much we want something and once we got it, how soon we lose our interest. I mean, don't get me wrong, it makes me sick, everything I lost that day. But it makes me wonder, too, seeing all those things destroyed, just what I spent my money on and what I could've had instead. (*Sighs.*) Anyway, once the sun goes down, that was another story. I never cared too much for night. Especially since my Henry died. And being alone with water up to my chin in a pitch-dark room, that's the worst night yet I ever passed. I start to imagine all kinds of things in the dark. You never heard a night more still. Nobody making any kind of noise. Nothing but the sloshing of the water. I got to stay awake, I got to stay awake, I got to stay awake, I tell myself. I don't know how I do it, but I do.

MARIE: You pray?

AMELIA: Oh, yeah, I try that for a little while. But tell the truth, there's not that much to say, you think you gonna die. You know, "Save me, God, and I'll be good." That kind of thing. What else is there to talk about? You make an act of contrition for all your sins. But you get to be a widow old as me, how long you think that takes? Turns out me and God, we sort of got this understanding, I guess. Something like me and Henry had. We could go for hours, he'd never open his mouth, just sit there reading his *Times-Picayune*. Don't God seem a lot like that to you? Off reading the paper and drinking a cup of coffee while you jabbering away in the kitchen.

MARIE: But how you manage to get out of there with the water up around your throat?

AMELIA: Well, I'll tell you. I'm stranded there like that all night and most of Tuesday morning. But then I hear a man outside start shouting from his boat: "Hey, anybody still alive in there?" "Yeah, mister, there's a lady trapped in here," I holler back. "Well, can you swim?" he wants to know. "All my life since I was small." "Then come on out. I'll take you to the overpass." So I pushed off toward the front door. By then, everything's so strange, I don't pay any attention to it— swimming across my living room, I mean. You ever hear of such a thing, a woman of my age, you have to swim through your own house to get outside? And when I come to the door, I got to dive underwater to get beneath the transom. I pop up right beside the boat, and the man, his name was Henry. How you like that for a coincidence? Same name as my own late husband, Henry. Almost like it was Henry come to save me, don't you think? Like my guardian angel or something. Well, Henry the boatman scoops me up out of that filthy water and gives me a can of beer to drink and takes me to the Interstate. We get there and, of course, that's when my troubles really start. But that's another story, darlin'.'

MARIE (*standing and leaning on the railing*): Trey's parents weren't so lucky.

AMELIA: I didn't want to ask. Them the "two dead" on the door?

MARIE: Yes, ma'am. Trapped up in the attic.

AMELIA: Lord, they still finding bodies in attics over where I used to live. Just found a man last month. A year after. You imagine that?

MARIE: Trey's taking it real bad, I think—first time being back here and all, I mean.

AMELIA: So this the very first time he come back?

MARIE: Well, we come to town to bury them last November.

AMELIA: Yeah, I went to quite a few funerals myself that month.

MARIE: I guess we should've come seen the place when we were over here for the burial, but tell you the truth, neither of us had the heart for it on top of the funeral and all. And we had work the next day back in Houston. Had to drive home that same night. Not to mention Trey forgot to bring the key.

AMELIA: But what about your own place? How'd you make out there?

MARIE: Oh, we just been married a few years. We were renting half a shotgun over in Gentilly.

AMELIA: You get much water?

MARIE: Just as bad as this. Lost everything.

AMELIA: Must be a shock, seeing how this looks now.

MARIE: Feels like yesterday, we're having dinner in the kitchen with Trey's mama and daddy, eating her pound cake with lemon sauce. Trey's favorite dessert. Wish I'd gotten that recipe from her.

(*TREY leaves the album and exits down the hallway.*)

AMELIA: How many family recipes lost in the flood?

(*Suddenly weak, MARIE feels for a chair and sits down.*)

You feeling all right, darlin'? You don't look so good.

MARIE: I'm just tired is all. Spent the whole night in the car driving over here.

AMELIA: Why y'all didn't come yesterday? Stay in a motel somewheres.

MARIE: You can't believe what they asking for a room around here now.

AMELIA: Yeah, well, the motels, they full up with people been living there since the flood. So they all charging two, three times what they were a year ago.

MARIE: We waited till after midnight—you know, let it cool off a little. Then we rolled the windows down and drove all night.

AMELIA: No air conditioner, huh?

MARIE: Went out on us last spring. I'll tell you, Mrs. Delachaise, that hot wind whipping me across the face for three hundred and fifty miles, I felt beat to death the time we got here this morning.

AMELIA: Yeah, I can see how pale you are.

MARIE: And breakfast didn't agree with me, the place we ate coming in.

AMELIA (*studying MARIE*): Mmmhmm. You all queasy in the stomach?

MARIE: It's the smell in there. It'd make anybody sick.

AMELIA: So this morning's the first time you get queasy?

MARIE: No, my stomach's been funny all week.

AMELIA: You all swoled up?

MARIE: The heat does that to me.

AMELIA: And you tender in your bosom?

MARIE (*cupping one of her breasts and nodding*): But I slept all twisted up last night in the car.

AMELIA: I think I know what you coming down with.

MARIE: Yeah, Trey says we both coming down with something.

AMELIA: Well, I don't know about your husband, but, girl, you coming down with a baby.

MARIE (*laughing*): A baby? No, I'm just tired is all.

AMELIA: You late, ain't you?

MARIE: Three weeks. But it's the worry. You know, what we were facing coming over here.

AMELIA: Honey child, trust me. You gonna be a mama.

MARIE: A mama?

AMELIA: It's a good thing, darlin.' Bringing a baby into this world, why it's the best thing you can do. My one regret in life, me and Henry never had a child.

MARIE: A child?

(*She puts her hand on her belly.*)

AMELIA (*taking the beer away from MARIE*): Tell me you don't feel pregnant.

MARIE (*her hand still on her belly*): I've been thinking I ought to pick up one of those tests when I'm at the store. But I keep putting it off.

AMELIA: Save your money, honey. There ain't no doubt.

MARIE: I've had these symptoms before.

AMELIA: All together?

MARIE: Well . . .

AMELIA: I'm happy for you, darlin.'

MARIE: I don't know this is a real good time for us to have a baby, though.

AMELIA: You think that baby of yours cares this a good time or not? Shit, all that baby cares is "Who's my mama gonna be?" And sure as I'm sitting here, that child's mama gonna be you.

(*TREY enters excitedly from the hallway.*)

MARIE: I don't know what Trey's gonna say.

TREY (*having just come onto the porch*): About what?

MARIE (*surprised*): Oh, Trey. Mrs. Delachaise was telling me she, uh . . .

AMELIA: Don't you put me in the middle of all this.

MARIE: She was saying she had the same idea as you did right after the flood. Fix up the house and move back in.

TREY: Well, I'll tell you, Mrs. Delachaise, I can see why you'd give up on your own house, an old lady like you—

AMELIA: I know you not starting with me again.

MARIE: Trey.

TREY: What?

(*MARIE nods toward AMELIA.*)

Oh. I mean, you know, not being able to rebuild the house by yourself and all, I mean. But us, we're gonna make this place look like new.

(*Holding open the screen door for them.*)

Come inside. Come see what I'm talking about.

MARIE: Trey.

TREY: Let me show you, Marie. Come on inside. I opened up some windows. It ain't so bad in there now.

MARIE: Don't you think you owe Mrs. Delachaise an apology?

TREY: For what?

AMELIA (*suddenly standing*): For what? You think I'm used to people talking to me like you did before.

TREY: It's just you show up out of the blue and start talking about knocking down our house—

MARIE: Your parents' house, Trey.

TREY: But that's what I want to show you, Marie. Come inside. Come see.

(*They enter the house, but AMELIA keeps MARIE between her and TREY.*)

MARIE: Trey, I already told Mrs. Delachaise we're selling the house and buying a place in Houston. You don't need to pretend—

TREY: But that's just it, Marie. We're not buying a place in Houston anymore.

MARIE: What are you talking about?

TREY: I'm sitting here looking through Mama's picture album I found. You know, photographs of Mama and Daddy at Pontchartrain Beach. Christmas pictures, me graduating from high school. When we got married, you and me. It's all in here.

MARIE: Yeah, I know, Trey, that's what photo albums are for. The past.

TREY: No, baby, these are photographs of the future.

MARIE: The future? What are you going on about, Trey?

TREY (*showing MARIE the album*): Look what I mean.

MARIE: These photos, they're all messed up from the water. Like they been scorched or something.

AMELIA: Folks call it the "Katrina patina," the stains all over your pictures.

MARIE: Well, we'll take the album with us. I'll see if I can clean them up when we get back home.

TREY: But that's what I realized, Marie. Looking at these pictures, I suddenly figured it out: we are home. *This* is our home.

AMELIA: You can't live here. Not the way it is.

TREY (*starts straightening up the room*): Yeah, I know. We gonna clean it all up. Brush off the mold. Put things back where they go. Sweep up.

AMELIA: You make it sound like all you need is a broom and a dust rag. Mister, you need a sledgehammer and a shovel to fix this place up.

TREY: It looks a lot worse than it really is.

AMELIA: No, you got that ass backwards, Mr. Guidry. It's really a lot worse than it looks. You can't feel those ridges under your feet where the water pushed up the floorboards? And you gonna need new wiring, insulation, sheetrock. And what about the gas lines all corroded from the saltwater?

TREY: That's just details you talking.

MARIE: We didn't drive all the way over here for any other reason than to settle the insurance and get a down payment for a house in Houston.

TREY: Yeah, maybe that's why we come. But being back here today, looking at those pictures, it couldn't be any clearer to me. *This* is our home. This is where we gonna live. You got to see that, Marie, don't you? This is where we supposed to live our lives. We'll be as happy as Mama and Daddy, you and me.

(*Tearing down the demolition notice.*)

So, Mrs. Delachaise, you can just scratch this address right off that list of houses you gonna knock down.

AMELIA: Wish I could, Mr. Guidry. But it's not as simple as people saying they want to come back home again. People been saying that ever since the flood, but where are they? You the first people I come across out here today.

TREY: It's Sunday. People at church, at home getting dinner ready.

AMELIA: I can tell you from experience, it wouldn't be all that different, I come out here tomorrow.

MARIE: She's right, Trey. Who's got the heart to come see their home like this, week after week? Your whole life, nothing but a pile of garbage sitting on the curb. What's left inside, all molded over. People just running out of steam.

TREY: Well, I got a full head of steam now when it comes to this house. And I'm not about to let Mrs. Delachaise knock it down.

AMELIA: I already explained it's not me, it's the city.

TREY: Yes, ma'am, but I'm not letting anyone—the city, I don't care who—come demolish this house. My parents lived here.

AMELIA: Your wife told me, Mr. Guidry. I'm real sorry for your loss. And I understand how you feel. People think you get old, you start to forget everything. But with me, it's just the opposite. It's like the past comes bleeding through the present all the time.

MARIE: Yeah, that's New Orleans, all right: always more concerned with the used to be than the gonna be. It's like living in the middle of a ghost story, living here.

AMELIA: Ooh, I don't like ghost stories. Night's bad enough without things like that running around in your head you try to sleep.

MARIE: You think this isn't some ghost town we in the middle of, Trey?

TREY: Baby—

MARIE: Go step out on that porch, Trey, and tell me what you see. A bunch of wrecked houses tumbling down on themselves. Their doors flung wide open, windows busted out. And not a human being anywhere in sight.

TREY: Sure, Marie, but—

MARIE (*stepping onto the porch*): And what do you hear, huh, standing on the porch? No babies crying, no mamas calling after their kids come in for lunch. No birds—

TREY: That don't make this a ghost town.

MARIE (*coming back inside*): You think we not the ghosts of what we were? You think we the same people we were a year ago?

TREY: Aw, you talking crazy, woman.

MARIE: You think all you got to do is rebuild this house and you'll get your old life back again.

AMELIA: She's right, Mr. Guidry. Fix this place up, you just pitching a tent in the middle of a graveyard.

TREY: I'm gonna get us back what we lost.

MARIE: You talk like some dead man don't yet know he's dead. Somebody just remembers being alive, that's all.

TREY: You just all stirred up coming over here today.

MARIE: You don't expect any minute now you'll hear your folks in the kitchen arguing whether the roast beef is done or not?

TREY: What you think home is but a house every corner's whispering a memory?

MARIE: And who's doing all that whispering in the corner, huh, Trey? Ghosts of things don't exist anymore.

AMELIA (*edging toward the door*): Perhaps it's time I be on my way.

(*Handing papers to MARIE.*)

I'll leave you some papers explain everything.

MARIE: Thank you.

AMELIA (*to TREY*): Look, I'm not putting you down on my demolition list. But y'all gonna have to do something. Another volunteer, somebody else gonna come around before long. They won't let you leave it like this, the house. Not in this condition.

TREY: Well, we appreciate your consideration, Mrs. Delachaise. And we gonna get started on it, don't you worry. Get this place cleaned up better than new.

MARIE: Let me see you out.

TREY (*as AMELIA and MARIE exit onto the porch*): When you come back in, Marie, I'll show you what we gonna do with the kitchen. I got it all worked out.

(*TREY continues to straighten up, carrying things into the hallway.*)

AMELIA (*on the porch*): Darlin', you can't bring a baby back to this house.

MARIE: I know. All that mold—

AMELIA: Yeah, you right, but that's not the thing I'm talking about. I mean, I ain't superstitious, but still, you can't raise a child in the same house its grandparents died in the attic. What you think that do to a little child goes to sleep every night staring at that ceiling?

MARIE: It's craziness, what he's thinking.

AMELIA: Your family in Texas?

MARIE: Yes, ma'am.

AMELIA: You need to be with your mama when you have that baby. This ain't no place for little children.

TREY (*shouting from inside, where he's still straightening up*): Marie. Oh, Marie, come see.

MARIE: Thank you, Mrs. Delachaise.

AMELIA (*hugging MARIE*): I'm real happy for you, honey. But you get your ass back home to Texas, you hear?

MARIE: Yes, ma'am.

AMELIA (*pointing to the ice chest*): Now you think I could have another one of those for the road?

(*MARIE hands her a beer. AMELIA pauses as she starts to exit and shouts to TREY in the house.*)

Bye, Mr. Guidry.

MARIE: You take care of yourself.

AMELIA (*as she exits*): Don't you worry about me, 'heart. You just take care of that baby of yours.

TREY (*shouting from inside*): Marie, come see. Let me show you what we gonna do.

MARIE: Yeah, I'm coming.

(*She doesn't move. Lights fade.*)

ACT II

(EDGAR, carrying a clipboard and with a tape measure on his belt, enters from the interior hallway, followed by TREY and MARIE. EDGAR continues to measure, sometimes with the help of TREY, and take notes as they talk.)

TREY: We should've never left it sealed up all this time. Should've aired the place out or something. But my wife's got family in Houston, so we evacuated to Texas the day before the storm. Been there ever since.

EDGAR: Y'all aren't the only ones haven't started gutting yet.

TREY: Woman come by just before you show up—some kind of volunteer or something—tells us the city's got a law says everybody's supposed to gut their houses by Tuesday. You believe that? Tuesday. But you don't think the city's really gonna hold people to that deadline, do you?

EDGAR: I've given up predicting what the city's gonna do. This one lady I spoke to, over on St. Anthony, her house is on some demolition list the city's got—public health hazard, imminent danger of collapse, something like that. A few weeks ago, she goes over to City Hall just to see what she needs to do to keep them from knocking down her house. But it's August, so the assessors got the tax rolls open. She figures as long as she's down there anyway, may as well check how much value her property's lost, what with the flood and all. Come to find out, though, the city's doubled the property's assessed value since last year— despite the fact they gonna bulldoze it first chance they get.

(He starts to laugh, but it turns into a cough.)

MARIE: You got that Katrina cough everybody's talking about.
EDGAR: It's the mold. The end of the day, I'm all raw up in here.

(He rubs his chest beneath his throat.)

The company says you don't need to worry about it, but I don't
know.
TREY: You got any tips on getting rid of it, the mold. Guess that's
the first thing I'm gonna have to do when we get started on this
place.
EDGAR: Well, before you do anything, go get yourself a decent
mask. And I'm not talking those little dust masks painters use.
You need the ones look like a gas mask. You know, got filters
on the bottom. They're hot as hell, but that's what you need.
You gonna want rubber gloves, too. And rubber boots wouldn't
hurt. It's a mess, getting rid of mold.
TREY: Guess I'll need some bleach, huh?
EDGAR: Don't bother with that. Bleach just makes mold harder
to see. The mold sends down these roots inside the wood. You
don't kill them, it comes right back. My house, after I finished
gutting the place, first thing I did, I took a wire brush to the
studs and vacuumed up the dust with a HEPA filter.
TREY: A what kind of filter?
EDGAR: HEPA. It filters out ninety-nine percent of what's in the air.
And I promise you, you don't want to breathe what's gonna get
in the air, you start cleaning this place. So keep that mask on.
TREY: But you kidding me, right? You didn't really scrape every
stud in your house?
EDGAR: Downstairs, anyway. Then I got this borate treatment—
expensive like you wouldn't believe—and brushed that on till it
soaked in. And finally, before we put up new sheetrock, I
encapsulated all the studs with this thick white paint kills mold
on contact in case it bloomed again once the weather got hot.

TREY: But that ain't all really necessary, is it? I mean, that's some job you talking about.

EDGAR: This old-timer the other side of Franklin Avenue—one of the first houses I got sent out on after the flood—he decides he's gonna rebuild. Three months, the place is ready to move in. But then, before he's even got any furniture, he starts to smell the mold still in the walls. So he tears out the new sheetrock in the laundry room, the kitchen, the bathroom—thinking it must be near the pipes, condensation, something like that. Sure enough, everywhere he looks, the studs are turning black again. And every room he walks into, he smells the spores in the air. So he rips open the walls in the living room and the dining room and the bedrooms. Time he's done, he's got nothing left but the studs, every one all black with mold. So he calls me up, says he's got a new problem, can I come see? I go out there, but I got to tell him we already paid you for what happened. We can't give you another check for damage you done yourself.

TREY: I had no idea.

EDGAR: They call it the fifth kingdom, mold.

MARIE: What they mean by that, the fifth kingdom?

EDGAR (*counting on his fingers*): You know, you got your bacteria, your one-celled creatures, your vegetable kingdom and your animals. But then you got this other kingdom. It's alive, but it don't ever move. Just sends out spores all the time, infecting everything else. That's the fifth kingdom—mold.

MARIE: Ought to just change the name of New Orleans to The Fifth Kingdom.

EDGAR: Me, I'm used to it now.

MARIE (*coughing*): Afraid I'm not.

EDGAR: No, it takes a while getting acclimated to it, the smell. So let's get this wrapped up, and you folks can be on your way.

(*Checking his clipboard.*)

You wouldn't happen to know the date of construction, would you?

TREY: Sorry?

EDGAR: When the house was built.

TREY: Oh. No, I'm not sure. The twenties, thirties, something like that, I'd guess.

EDGAR: No problem. I can look it up.

(*Continuing to check his clipboard.*)

Let's see. And the stove, that was gas, not electric, right?

MARIE: Yeah, gas. The oven, too.

EDGAR: OK, I still need to take a look at the roof. Let me go get the ladder from my truck and climb up there.

TREY: Give you a hand?

EDGAR: Nah, thanks. I can manage.

(*EDGAR exits.*)

MARIE: What are we doing, Trey?

TREY: What do you mean what are we doing? We gonna get a big fat check from the insurance company, fix this place up, and make it our home. We gonna get our lives back again, Marie.

MARIE: Tell me how we're gonna turn all this back into a normal life again?

(*TREY starts hauling out trash from the house and piling it outside, then continues to straighten up the room as they talk.*)

TREY: You just can't see what we gonna have once we done rebuilding.

MARIE: And you can't see what's right in front of your eyes. Look at this place.

TREY: So what would you rather we do?

ARIE: Do what Mrs. Delachaise did.

TREY: Knock it down, the house? And then what?

MARIE: It's been a year since the storm, and how many people come back so far?

TREY: People coming back all the time.

MARIE: Coming back to what? No place to live, no jobs left, the schools in shambles. Why would anyone come back here?

TREY: Because it's New Orleans.

MARIE: And what's that mean?

TREY: Happiness. I showed you that poll they took last summer before the flood. New Orleans was the happiest city in the country.

MARIE: And what did we have to be so happy about, this city? Got some of the worst schools in the South, it's the murder capital of the country, our politicians steal us blind, the housing for the poor people, we ought to be ashamed. So what were we so damn happy about down here, huh?

TREY: You just don't like New Orleans anymore.

MARIE: I hate this goddamn city.

TREY: Well, you weren't born here.

MARIE: Yeah, you New Orleanians, you love this godforsaken place, don't you?

TREY: Can't ever explain to someone it's not home for, why we love it.

MARIE: All you talking about, you put up with things nobody else in his right mind would live with.

TREY: The time I'm done with this place, you won't have nothing to put up with. It'll be perfect, our home. You'll see. But hang on a minute.

(*He steps onto the porch and shouts to EDGAR on the roof.*)

Hey, so how's it look up there? I can come up and give you a hand.

EDGAR (*from the roof*): No, I'm fine. I'll be down in a minute.

TREY: Well, you holler if you need me.

(*He gets another beer from the cooler before coming back inside to finish straightening the room and to continue his conversation with MARIE.*)

We get our money and make this place look like new, you'll feel real different about everything, you'll see. You just tired now is all.

MARIE: Sick and tired of living in a city full of problems even before all its houses looked like this.

TREY (*plops onto the straightened sofa and puts his feet up, sipping his beer*): It's not so bad, the city.

MARIE: Not so bad? We haven't been back here two hours, and what've we seen? Streets collapsing underneath the car, the whole place looking like a war zone, soldiers everywhere you turn.

TREY: They just here to keep you safe.

MARIE: I don't want to live in a city it takes an army to keep me safe.

TREY: It hasn't been a year since the flood went down.

MARIE: And people no better off now than they were then. Still no police, no hospitals, no mail—

TREY: You got to look at the bright side of things.

MARIE: Bright side? Look around you right here, Trey. You sitting in your parents' own house, the house you grew up in. This don't make you sick to death, this place?

TREY: It's not so bad. Once you get used to it.

MARIE: I don't want to get used to it. You can't feel it in your chest, the mold, down in your lungs, deep inside you?

TREY: Yeah, but I'm outside a few minutes, it goes away.

MARIE: That's not how normal people live, you got to go outside to get away from what the inside does to you.

(*MARIE angrily exits onto the porch as EDGAR enters.*)

EDGAR (*entering the house*): She OK?

TREY: Yeah, she's had this stomach virus all week, nauseous all the time.

EDGAR: Seems like a lot of people sick around here.

TREY: So what you got for me?

EDGAR: Well, the roof's in pretty good shape. A few tiles missing, that's all.

TREY: So that's good, huh?

EDGAR (*paging through forms on his clipboard*): Yeah, you're OK up there. But I can still give you a little wind damage on the roof, maybe count that length of fence fell over out front— though tell you the truth, probably was the flood knocked that down. And the back door's stove in; most likely the soldiers kicked it in searching for survivors. I seen a lot of that.

TREY: Couldn't get past the deadbolt on the front door.

EDGAR: Well, we can't tell one way or another what happened, so, yeah, let's call that wind damage, too. But I don't see much else the storm did.

TREY: No, it was the flood did the real damage, not the hurricane.

EDGAR: Exactly.

TREY: What about the car in the driveway?

EDGAR: That's not covered under homeowner's. That's auto.

(*He checks a form.*)

And the automobile policy y'all had didn't include comprehensive.

TREY: So what? You insured the car, and the car's a total loss.

EDGAR: But you had collision, not comprehensive. Now if the car had been in a wreck—

TREY: The car's been in worse than a wreck. There's no fixing a car been under water for two weeks.

EDGAR: Yes, sir, that's true. But it wasn't covered for flood.

TREY: So, wait. You saying we don't get anything for the car?

EDGAR: Sorry.

TREY: But that can't be right. The car's ruined. I mean, go see what I'm talking about. The mold's so thick it looks like dirty cotton balls stuck to the inside of the windows. And the paint job—it's all pocked with rust from the saltwater.

EDGAR: Yes, sir, you're absolutely right. It's totaled, the car. But what I'm trying to explain is it wasn't covered for flood.

TREY: So nothing? You won't pay nothing on it?

EDGAR: I'm sorry, no.

TREY: Well, can you tow it away, at least? Get it out the driveway. That's where I'm gonna put the trailer when we start rebuilding.

EDGAR: You and your wife gonna live in one of those FEMA trailers?

TREY: Yeah, I think so. Till we get the house fixed up.

EDGAR: Kind of cramped, the trailers I been in. And hot like you wouldn't believe. Can't use the stove, it heats up the place so bad.

TREY: I'm a New Orleanian. I can take the heat.

EDGAR: Every one I been in, people got tinfoil taped over the windows and bathroom towels tacked up over the curtains to keep the heat out.

TREY: Well, it's not comfort we looking for. Just a place to stay while I rebuild this house.

EDGAR: On the other hand, you'll be lucky if you get a trailer, let me tell you. They got people driving in from Baton Rouge every day 'cause they can't find a place here to stay. Hell, we got adjustors from out of state, three or four sharing one room out past Gonzales. They making more money from mileage than from salary.

TREY: So you help me out and tow the car out of the driveway at least?

EDGAR: Afraid we can't do that. Not unless the car had comprehensive.

TREY: Yeah, which it don't. (*He sighs.*) Man, I was counting on that money to get a new car. The one we driving's falling apart. You sure there's nothing you can do?

EDGAR: Without comprehensive . . .

TREY: OK. Forget the damn car. (*Pause.*) So how much we talking for the house? I mean, it's as bad as the car. Worse. So you gonna total the house like you would've the car?

EDGAR: Like I said before, you've got minimal damage from the hurricane itself.

TREY: Yeah, most of this, it's all from the levees collapsing.

EDGAR: So you're not looking at much for wind damage.

TREY: Right, but the flood damage, it's got to be thousands and thousands of dollars.

EDGAR: Oh, easy. You count contents, you probably talking at least a hundred thousand dollars damage here. And you factor in what contractors are charging right now—just what you got to pay for copper tubing, you won't believe—you could be looking at, I don't know, a hundred and fifty thousand before you're done.

TREY: A hundred fifty thousand dollars? That's way more than we were hoping for.

EDGAR: I got people turned in estimates by contractors of fifteen thousand just to gut their places. Of course, the company won't pay that much for gutting—the customer just gets the regional average—but that's what some contractors are asking here in New Orleans.

TREY: Fifteen thousand dollars to rip out sheetrock?

EDGAR: And just try to find somebody to do it, too. People wait six, eight weeks for a work crew.

TREY: Yeah, well, me and Marie gonna gut the place ourselves.

EDGAR: That's what I did over at my house.

TREY: I'd just as soon put that fifteen grand in my own pocket as pay someone else.

(*Pause.*)

So, Mr. Bernard, how soon can we expect the money. With a hundred fifty thousand dollars, I'll turn this house into a palace.

EDGAR: I'm sorry, but I think you're confused, Mr. Guidry. I was talking about what it would cost, not what you're going to get.

TREY: Yeah, yeah, I know. We get the regional average, like you said. But still, that's got to be a lot money. I mean, look at this place.

EDGAR: Yes, sir, that's true. But everything here, it wasn't the wind did this.

TREY: No, it was the water. The levees collapsing. The goddamn Corps of Engineers.

EDGAR: Exactly. But your homeowner's policy only covers wind, fire, things like that.

TREY: Yeah, in case the house gets destroyed. Like what happened here.

EDGAR: Well, but that's the point. It's not for what happened here. For this kind of damage, you need flood insurance.

(*Checking more forms.*)

And according to my records, the house isn't insured for flood.

TREY: What are you talking about?

EDGAR: According to the records I got here, you're not covered for flood.

TREY: Not covered?

EDGAR: Maybe we ought get Mrs. Guidry involved in this conversation so I can explain it to her, too.

TREY (*shouting*): Marie. Hey, Marie, come hear this, what he's saying, this man.

EDGAR (*moving toward the door*): Why don't we go out on the porch and get some fresh air?

MARIE (*at the door*): You call me?

TREY: You stay there. We coming out.

(*To EDGAR, having exited onto the porch with him.*)

Now tell my wife what you just told me.

EDGAR: I was trying to explain to your husband that most of what happened here, it's not wind caused the damage.

TREY: Anybody takes one look at this place can see that.

EDGAR: So most of the damage to your house isn't covered under your homeowner's policy.

MARIE: This isn't our house, Mr. Bernard. This is my husband's parents' home.

EDGAR (*to TREY, confused*): I'm sorry. I thought you said you were Emile Guidry.

TREY: I am. But it's my father's name, too. I only go by Emile for legal things—things like this. People call me Trey.

EDGAR: Maybe it would be best if I spoke directly to the policyholders.

MARIE: Trey's mama and daddy got trapped in the attic. (*Pause.*) When the water came up.

EDGAR: They're deceased, the policyholders?

TREY: Who you think those "2 dead" are on the door there?

EDGAR: I've seen so many of those X's, I didn't even notice it. I'm sorry for your loss, Mr. Guidry. I should've realized; there's probably a note in here somewhere. I just got the file this morning.

MARIE: This morning? We set up this meeting two weeks ago.

EDGAR: Yes, ma'am, but I'm covering for another adjustor was assigned this property originally. He got transferred Friday, and they told me to take all his appointments this weekend.

TREY: But tell my wife what you told me.

EDGAR: I was explaining to your husband that, according to our records, there hasn't been a flood policy written on this property since . . .

(*He checks his files.*)

Since 2002.

MARIE: That's about when Trey's parents paid off their mortgage. Two, three years ago, right, Trey? His mama made a cake in the shape of the house to celebrate, they were so proud.

EDGAR: That makes sense. Without a mortgage, they wouldn't have been required to carry flood insurance.

TREY: And why should they? They lived here thirty-something years—I don't know how many hurricanes they been through—and water never once even got up over the curb.

EDGAR: That may be, Mr. Guidry, but all this, it's not wind damage. This is all rising water.

MARIE: Sounds like your daddy, don't it, Trey, canceling his flood insurance? He wasn't one to pay for something he never thought he'd ever need.

EDGAR: But I'm afraid without flood coverage, there's not much I can do.

TREY: So this is just like the damn car, huh? They got insurance, all right, but not the kind you pay anything when there's a claim.

MARIE: Their car wasn't insured?

TREY: Oh, yeah. They had plenty of car insurance. Just not the right kind. Ain't that so, Mr. Bernard?

EDGAR: I'm afraid they didn't carry comprehensive.

MARIE: And the house is the same deal? You're saying it don't apply, their insurance?

EDGAR: Not as far as I can tell. Now you provide a certificate of flood insurance, I'll be happy to—

TREY: Where we get that?

EDGAR: Your parents would probably have a copy with their insurance papers.

TREY (*entering the house*): What you think their papers gonna look like, I even find them somewhere in all this mess the flood left?

EDGAR (*entering the house, followed by MARIE*): Yes, sir, I understand. And before you go looking, I haven't had a case yet, our records were wrong.

TREY: The damn Corps of Engineers knew how to build a levee, my father never would have seen any water in his house.

EDGAR: And I'm afraid without flood insurance—

TREY: But his house insurance, something, must kick in, huh? Cover some of this at least.

EDGAR: Well, sure, like I said, we'll cover repairing the roof and the fence and the back door.

MARIE: But that's all?

EDGAR: Without flood coverage—

TREY: So what? They got homeowner's insurance. And this is
their home.

EDGAR: But that's not how it works.

TREY: It can't be we lose everything and you don't pay nothing.

EDGAR: No, you gonna get something for the roof and the fence—

TREY: And the back door. Yeah, yeah, I get that. But what else?

EDGAR: Else?

TREY: I mean, what else are you gonna pay for?

EDGAR: That's what I'm telling you. The only damage their policy
covers is the roof and the fence—

TREY: Yeah, and their fuckin' back door. But you can't mean that's
it. You said we got a hundred fifty thousand dollars' worth of
damage here.

EDGAR: But it's not wind damage. (*Pause.*) And I should tell you,
the fact your parents died, that could complicate things. Since
they were the actual policyholders, I mean.

TREY: My parents pay you premiums for better than thirty years
on a house all in ruins now, and you won't pay for nothing but
a few roof tiles, a length of fence, and a new back door? And
on top of that, since they dead, you may not pay anything at
all? How about you just return those thirty years of premiums,
and we'll call it square?

EDGAR: That's not what I said, Mr. Guidry. It's just, we can't
release payment to anyone other than the policyholder.
But, look, I got forms here. You fill them out and submit the
documents they got listed there, this'll all work out. Just take
a little time, that's all.

TREY: How you live with yourself? Treating people this way.

EDGAR: I'm doing everything I can for you, sir. It's not my fault
your parents didn't carry flood insurance.

TREY: It's like a goddamn shell game, what you do. Whatever
happens, we got the wrong kind of insurance. Yeah, your car's
insured—just not for this. Yeah, you got house insurance, but
we don't cover the way your house just got destroyed. No, you

need some other kind of insurance your house gets destroyed
that way.

EDGAR: I'm sorry, Mr. Guidry, but the rules are the rules. And the
company's not bending those rules for anybody right now.

TREY: You know what I think of your fuckin' goddamn rules?

MARIE: So you have an estimate for us yet, Mr. Bernard?

TREY: Next to nothing, that's what the son of a bitch is offering.

EDGAR: That's not what I said, Mr. Guidry.

TREY: So tell my wife how much you talking about then.

EDGAR: Somebody else decides that, not me.

TREY: But give her some idea.

EDGAR: My guess—and it's nothing but a guess, you understand—
you're looking at a couple thousand.

MARIE: Two thousand dollars? That's all? But the city wants to
knock it down there's so much damage.

EDGAR: It's just an estimate, but yeah, about two thousand,
probably. Of course, that's before the deductible.

MARIE: And how much is that?

EDGAR: Let me see.

(*He checks the file.*)

Five hundred. But you're only gonna get eighty percent of what we
owe you. You don't get the rest until you finish rebuilding.

MARIE: So . . .

EDGAR (*he pulls out a calculator*): Two thousand minus a five
hundred dollar deductible times eighty percent . . . It comes to
a thousand, two hundred dollars.

TREY: Twelve hundred dollars? That's all we gonna get?

EDGAR: It's only an estimate, Mr. Guidry. Could be a little more.

TREY: Or could be a little less.

EDGAR: Yeah, could be. I've got no control over how much they
give you. Someone else figures that out.

TREY: So ain't none of you responsible. It's always somebody else
makes the decisions.

EDGAR: I keep trying to explain, that's how insurance works.

TREY: Well, explain to me how I'm supposed to rebuild this house for twelve hundred dollars?

EDGAR: I were you, I'd get myself over to one of those salvage yards off Carrollton Avenue. You can pick up a back door matches what you had here for next to nothing.

TREY: Salvage yard?

EDGAR: Yeah, then you go over to Home Depot. They got fencing real cheap you can use to fix that section the water knocked down.

TREY: What are you talking about?

EDGAR: Just do it yourself. When I was up there, the roof felt real solid. Wouldn't take much to replace the shingles got blown off.

MARIE: But the floors are all buckled, the plumbing, the wiring—

EDGAR: Oh, yes, ma'am, you talking quite a job, all right.

MARIE: And, Trey, you don't know the first thing about carpentry, rewiring a house—

EDGAR: You run into any problems, there's plenty of people willing to give you a hand.

MARIE: Like who?

EDGAR: Well, they got a bunch of religious groups helping out. Mennonite Disaster Services, Catholic Charities.

TREY: Mennonites?

EDGAR: Oh, they're something, those people. Do a hell of a job.

TREY: They don't even drive cars, Mennonites.

EDGAR: That's maybe the Amish you thinking of. And they not the only ones, the Mennonites. A busload of Episcopalians or Evangelicals or some other church group'll show up eventually and give you a hand gutting the place. They down here every weekend, volunteer groups like that. Just get yourself on one of their lists.

MARIE: One of their lists? This house ain't remediated by Tuesday, the city says it's gonna come bulldoze the place.

EDGAR: I'm afraid there's nothing I can do about that, Mrs. Guidry, but look, the government's got this program for people can't afford to rebuild on their own.

MARIE: It's the government wants to demolish the house.

EDGAR: Yeah, well, this is the state, not the city, I'm talking about.

TREY: And how long it takes to get your money from the government?

EDGAR: Well, there's no guarantee you'll get any money, especially since the original property owners are deceased.

TREY: But how long?

EDGAR: I hear it's taking about six months to get an interview to find out if you qualify to apply. Then once you submit all the paperwork, I don't know, maybe a year or so after that to get any money. They call it the Road Home program.

MARIE: That's one damn long road home.

EDGAR: But it's something, at least.

TREY: And you're really something, too, aren't you?

EDGAR: I'm sorry.

TREY: You show up with your tape measure and your clipboard and all those forms like you here to help people lost everything.

EDGAR: That's exactly what I'm here for.

TREY: To help us, huh?

EDGAR: That's right. Insurance is complicated business. I'm here to see you get every penny you deserve.

TREY: And that comes to twelve hundred dollars.

EDGAR: Look, I gave you a new back door when we both know it was the soldiers kicked it in. The fence, too. That wasn't the wind knocked it down. Another adjustor wouldn't 've given you anything but the roof.

TREY: So I'm supposed to say thank you for twelve hundred dollars?

EDGAR: Just saying you walking away with more than you probably deserve.

TREY: More than I deserve?

EDGAR: I went by the book, yeah.

TREY: You're from down here, ain't you?

EDGAR: I've been a New Orleanian all my life.

TREY: So you nothing but a goddamn traitor.

EDGAR: Traitor? You know what kind of days I've been working for a year now getting folks their money? Twelve, fifteen hours. If it wasn't for people like me, this city would be dead.

TREY: It's people like you killing this city.

EDGAR: Yeah? Well where you been for the last year?

TREY (*overlapping with the next line by EDGAR*): How much overtime you pulling down for all those hours you working, huh?

EDGAR (*overlapping with the next line by TREY*): You didn't see me run away. I stayed here and helped people.

TREY: Oh yeah, making sure they got all the money they deserved, huh?

EDGAR: No, I'm talking the week the levees collapsed. Know what I did while you were having coffee with your in-laws over in Texas? I waded in water up to my chest, got my fishing boat out, and started pulling people off their rooftops. Mothers with little babies. Old women all dehydrated from the heat. This big family—aunts, uncles, cousins—so many I had to make three trips to ferry them all to high ground. The whole week with me shouting, "Anybody there? Anybody hear me?" And most the time, the only answer I get is some poor dog barking, some poor dog people left behind when they evacuated to Texas just like you. I went everywhere I could get to trying to save people. I probably passed this house.

TREY: This house?

EDGAR (*sinking onto a chair*): It was hard to tell where I was with the water up to the roofs. But yeah, I was somewhere around here toward the end of the week. That family I saved wasn't far from here.

TREY: And you didn't hear nobody calling for help when you passed by?

EDGAR: Dogs barking maybe. I'd heard any people, I would've done something. But no, the only people I heard that evening was that big family on their roof.

TREY: You sure you never heard nobody when you come past this house in your boat that night?

EDGAR: No, but that was Thursday evening already. You talking a good three days after the levees crumbled.

TREY: Well, that don't mean there weren't people still alive.

EDGAR: Yeah, that family was still alive.

TREY: But you didn't hear nobody else yelling for help, making some kind of noise when you go past here?

EDGAR: I would've done something if I had.

TREY: If it'd been me, I would've checked every single house. See if I couldn't save some people.

EDGAR: I did save some people.

TREY: But the ones hard to find, I'm talking about. The ones too weak to make any noise.

EDGAR: Then how would I know they were even there?

TREY: I'm just saying, it would've been me with a boat—

EDGAR (*standing up to confront TREY*): But you weren't in a boat, were you? You were sitting in some air-conditioned room in Texas watching it all on the TV.

MARIE (*trying to defuse the argument*): Mr. Bernard, we shouldn't keep you. Mr. Bernard. You have other appointments.

(*Pause.*)

EDGAR: Yeah, I got one over in Lakeview.

(*He tosses forms on a chair and starts to leave but then stops.*)

I saved a lot of people that week. A lot of people.

(*EDGAR exits.*)

TREY (*picking up something and hurling it against the sofa*): That son of a bitch.

MARIE: You OK?

TREY: One tells me she's gonna knock the house down if I don't fix it up, and the other won't give me the money so I can.

MARIE: Trey, I know this is your parents' house and all, but—

TREY: Don't worry, baby. The hell with insurance. We'll manage without the money.

MARIE: Manage how? You don't see how much work there is to do here?

TREY: I'm not afraid of a little hard work.

MARIE: I'm not talking about work, Trey. I'm talking about money. How we gonna afford to do the first thing over here?

TREY: Little by little, we'll get it done.

MARIE: Little by little? You don't hear those bulldozers coming down the street?

TREY: I can't just turn my back on all this. My daddy didn't raise me to walk away, things get hard.

MARIE: But the floors, the wiring, the sheetrock, the furniture— how we gonna pay for all this? This is crazy, Trey. Those are good wages we're making in Texas. Where we gonna make that kind of money down here?

TREY: I'm a New Orleanian, Marie. You knew that when you married me. This whole year, it's been like living in another country, living someplace else.

MARIE: But there's nowhere here for us to live.

TREY: Sure there is. We gut one of the bedrooms first, do whatever we got to do to get rid of the mold. Then sand the floor and hang some sheetrock. Get a bed in there, we're all set.

MARIE: What about electricity? What about a bathroom?

TREY: Yeah, yeah. All that, too. And then the rest. The kitchen, whatever you want. We're gonna get started on it this morning, right this very minute—

MARIE: Are you out of your mind? Stay here? We got jobs back home.

TREY: That's not back home, Marie. *This* is back home.

MARIE: You got—what?—a year to get this place to where we could even sleep here.

TREY: No way. A month—a couple weeks—I could have that bedroom done. Come see. Let me show you what I'm gonna do.

(*TREY takes MARIE by the hand and leads her around.*)

Over here, we're gonna knock out this wall. Make the living room bigger. Then between the kitchen and the dining room, we put in a half wall with columns holding up the ceiling. Make everything real airy the way you like.

MARIE: Trey, how we gonna afford all this with twelve hundred dollars of insurance?

TREY (*ignoring her question*): And maybe we add a bathroom off our bedroom. And we make the closet bigger.

MARIE: How can we go without you bringing home a paycheck while you do all this? We ain't got any savings, not after this last year.

TREY: Aw, baby—

MARIE: Don't you "Aw, baby" me. I stay in here another minute, I'll suffocate. Makes me sick to my stomach, how it smells.

TREY: You can't expect me let 'em knock down my daddy's house. Let 'em crush my mama's furniture.

MARIE: They're gone, Trey, your mama and daddy. You make this house look like new, they still ain't coming back.

TREY: And you, you just want to lock the door and walk away?

MARIE: Walk away? You think it don't kill me, what went on in this house?

TREY: This whole past year, the longer it goes, the less I feel it's me walking around. It's like I'm watching someone else living my life.

MARIE: And you think you stay here longer, it's gonna get better? You think you gonna find yourself buried somewhere here in all these ruins?

TREY: Well, I ain't gonna find myself somewhere I never been.

MARIE: You don't see you stay here, the mold's gonna cover you over just like it's done everything else?

TREY: What would you think of a husband, he'd abandon his home and run away?

MARIE: He run away with his wife, I'd think he loves that woman more than he loves whatever's keeping him here.

TREY: That's the choice you giving me? My wife or my home?

MARIE: Your wife is your home, Trey. You don't know that by now, after what we been through this year . . .

(*MARIE starts to exit onto the porch.*)

TREY: A wife don't walk out on her husband, Marie.

MARIE (*coming back inside*): I'll be your wife anywhere you want but here.

TREY: You think even if I go, I won't carry all this with me?

MARIE: I can make you forget this place.

TREY: Forget? What's left of me, I forget all this? We go someplace else, I'll be a stranger the rest of my life.

MARIE: You didn't hesitate, ask me be a stranger here all these years.

TREY: Stranger? My parents didn't treat you like a daughter? That's my grandma's wedding ring on your finger. Only thing my mama got left of her own mother, and who she gives it to but you? And Daddy, you know what he tells me the day we get married? He say you ever lay a hand on that girl in anger, boy, I'll come find you where you live and beat you down one side of the street and up the other. My father, he takes up for you before you even need taking up for. You think they didn't love you like their own, my mama and daddy?

MARIE: I ain't saying otherwise, Trey. But I followed you here 'cause I love you. And now it's time you follow me.

TREY: My family been here over a hundred years. This place is who I am.

MARIE: No, Trey, this place is who you used to be. But look at it now. Look at this mold, the roots so deep in everything, you can't ever dig it all out.

TREY: But that's the way New Orleans is in me, too. How deep you think those roots go? Think they don't run deeper than what happened?

MARIE: Trey, we can't come back here.

TREY (*furiously*): I'm done talking with you about this. I'm gonna fix up this house, and we're moving back here to live. And that is final. I don't want to hear another word. You're not talking me into running away again like you did last time. I never should've listened to you. I should have stayed here and—

MARIE: I'm pregnant, Trey.

TREY: What?

MARIE (*exiting onto the porch*): I'm pregnant.

TREY (*following MARIE onto the porch*): Pregnant? What are you talking about, pregnant?

MARIE: We're gonna have a baby.

TREY: We never talked about you getting pregnant.

MARIE: It wasn't talk got me this way.

TREY: Anyway, you can't have a baby. The car needs an air conditioner.

MARIE: What?

TREY: I mean how we gonna pay for a baby? We need all kinds of things before we start talking baby.

MARIE: Things are way past the talking stage when it comes to this child.

TREY: But—

MARIE: There ain't no but, Trey. I'm gonna be a mama. You're gonna be a daddy. And we're gonna have a baby.

TREY: But why you wait until this morning to tell me all this? This ain't how you break the news to a man.

MARIE: Break the news? Trey, honey, this ain't some tragedy we're talking about. This is the best news you're ever gonna get in your whole damn life.

TREY: Yeah, well, I'm happy.

MARIE: You don't sound happy.

TREY: I got other stuff on my mind this morning. And now is when you choose to tell me something like this?

MARIE: I didn't choose this morning. I didn't choose to get pregnant. I didn't choose your parents to die in this house, this city to be destroyed. Choice has got nothing to do with any of it. And I only just realized this morning why I've been feeling this way . . . You're not happy we're gonna be a family?

TREY: Sure, sure I am. It's just a surprise, you springing it on me this way. (*Pause.*) But it's all the more reason we need to stay here. I'm not raising my child somewhere else.

MARIE: No, no, it's all the more reason we can't possibly stay here. Where are we going to live, for one thing? Even if you could fix this place up somehow without money, how long is it going to take to have a house to live in?

TREY: I'm gonna get us a trailer for the driveway.

MARIE: There's no room for a baby in those trailers.

TREY: Babies don't take up any space.

MARIE: Yeah, but you feed them, they grow.

TREY: Not right away. They real slow growing at first. And the time he needs a room, this place'll be done.

MARIE: This ain't a city for little children, Trey. My friend Angelique told me the other day on the phone she got her kid in the second grade at some Catholic school here. And her little boy's teacher told her every time it rained this spring, the children started crying. Then for Easter, the class drew crayon pictures of their families to hang up in the room. Except nobody puts the family on the lawn or in the doorway or even in the windows of the house. Every child in the class, they draw their families on the roof.

TREY: A few years, they'll be OK, those kids.

MARIE: I wonder, Trey. Wonder if anybody come back whole from what went on here.

TREY: Wait a few months, the old folks get back, the kids, see it don't feel like it always did.

MARIE: This ain't any place to bring a child back to. All those poisons the water left in the ground where children play—the pesticides, the gasoline, the mercury.

TREY: But these kids we still got here, they know something about this world a whole lot of grownups don't. And they'll never regret they know it, either, these children.

MARIE: Yeah, you men all for lessons leave a child in tears.

TREY: My father was done beating me, he always used to say, "Better you cry now than later."

MARIE: You think you ever gonna impress a woman telling her tears are good for children? Impress us a whole lot more, you tell us about all the tears you'll keep our kids from shedding.

TREY: You think I like it? You think I like those babies draw their families on the roof? But I'm the third one in a row in our family named Emile. You know that's why they call me Trey. And our little Emile gonna be the fourth. Right here in the same house I grew up in.

MARIE: You can't raise a child in this house.

TREY (*entering the house*): Sure we can. In the baby's room, little Emile's room, I'll put in new windows overlook the backyard. So it won't be so dark in there.

MARIE (*still on the porch*): There's no way on God's earth I'm raising a child in there.

TREY (*inside*): There's nothing wrong with this house we can't fix. And my son is not growing up somewhere else. Grow up talking like he's from somewhere else. No way.

MARIE (*following TREY into the house*): You're not listening to me, Trey. We can't raise our child here.

TREY: Marie, my parents are never gonna get to see their grandchild. And you know they wanted that more than anything else in the world. How often they tease you, "Where's our grandbaby?" How often you hear them say that?

MARIE: They're gone, Trey, your parents.

TREY: Yeah, you think I don't know they're gone?

MARIE: I don't know, Trey. Every time I try to talk with you about what happened here, you go open another beer and turn on the TV.

TREY: Well, what's there to say, Marie? You make me drive you to Texas 'cause a storm's coming, so I leave my parents here to die all alone in their attic.

MARIE: We begged them to come, Trey.

(*Pause.*)

And your mama wanted to go.

TREY: We stood right here in this living room, and when we asked them come with us to Houston, she never opened her mouth.

MARIE: Yeah, but when she and I went in the kitchen, she told me it was up to her, they'd be going with us.

TREY: She never said no such thing.

MARIE: No, not with your father leaning back in his chair insisting they weren't going anywhere "for some damn hurricane."

TREY: And he was right. The levees hadn't collapsed, he would've been laughing at us two days later when we come back.

MARIE: But the levees did collapse, Trey. You've got to open your eyes. Baby, look at this place. It's not a home. It's not even a house anymore. It's something you need to bury.

TREY: Bury?

(*He looks up at the ceiling.*)

Bury? You think my daddy'd want me to just turn my back and walk away?

MARIE: How'd they identify the bodies, the soldiers found your parents in the attic?

TREY: What's that got to do with staying or going?

MARIE (*cornering TREY and holding him there with her hand*): Your daddy found some duct tape up the attic and what did he do with it?

(*Pause.*)

Taped your mama's driver's license to her arm. Then he did the same thing to himself. Why you think he did that?

(*Pause.*)

'Cause the attic must have been a hundred thirty degrees up there and he knew nobody was coming to save them.

(*Pause.*)

What you think that's like? Taping your wife's name to her body 'cause you know the two of you gonna die and there's nothing you can do about it. Imagine taping my name to me so after I die my body can be identified.

(*Pause.*)

But why? Why your daddy do that, huh? Something terrible as that.

(*Pause.*)

So we wouldn't think when the water went down maybe they were still alive somewhere. He didn't want your mama and him to turn into two ghosts haunting us the rest of our lives. He wanted us to be able to bury them and move on.

(*Pause.*)

You worried what would your daddy expect of you? He'd expect you be the kind of man he was and face up to the situation we in.
TREY: I'm not running away again, Marie. I run away once, and my parents died. I'm not doing that again.

MARIE: You stay here, that's exactly what you're doing—running away.

TREY: Running away? From what?

MARIE: From your life. From me. Don't you see your pregnant wife standing here begging you let's go home?

TREY: This is our home.

MARIE: No, this is some awful thing happened a year ago you couldn't stop then and you can't change now.

TREY: I listened to you last time, and my parents die.

MARIE: You couldn't save your parents, Trey. Nobody could've saved them once that water come up. What could you've done your daddy didn't do?

TREY (*at the foot of the attic stairs*): You don't understand.

MARIE: Understand what? You did everything you could.

TREY: No, I didn't.

(*Pause.*)

I could've made them get in that car and come with us. But my daddy started laughing at me, and I backed down. Just like I always did. "Go on and run away," he said. "And see you not back here in two days looking like some goddamn fool scared away by a little rain."

(*Pause, then looking up the attic stairs.*)

I could've made you get in that car. I could've told you, "Get your ass in that car," and you would've done it. You would've done what I said.

MARIE: You tried—

TREY: No, I backed down just like I always did.

MARIE: That's not true.

TREY: I left my mama to die with him up in that attic 'cause I wasn't man enough to stand up to him.

MARIE: Baby, he was never leaving. Never. You would've had to drag him out of here and stuff him in the car.

TREY: Then why didn't I? Why didn't I pull that hardheaded son of a bitch out of his chair and drag his ass to the car like Mama wanted?

MARIE: Because he was your father, Trey. You can't go on blaming yourself—

TREY: Well, who else is there left to blame for what went on here?

MARIE: Blame the men who built those useless goddamn levees. Blame those jackasses in Washington who didn't send help for a week. But you do not blame yourself for something you couldn't stop. You told him come with us, but he wouldn't listen.

TREY: He never listened to nobody that man.

MARIE (*she goes weak and sinks onto the sofa*): Just like you not listening to me now.

TREY (*turning away from the attic and toward MARIE*): What's the matter? You OK?

(*MARIE shakes her head no.*)

What are you doing there? It's filthy, that sofa. Come on, get up off of there. Let's get you out on the porch.

(*TREY struggles to help MARIE onto the porch and into a chair. MARIE drops her head into her hands as if about to faint. TREY pours the water from a bottle over his hands to clean them, then pours more water, wiping MARIE's neck and face with his damp hands. She looks up at him and grasps his shirt, pulling him down. He kneels and holds her, her head cradled in his arm as he strokes her hair.*)

It's gonna be OK, baby. I promise. It's gonna be all right.

(*Lights fade.*)

NOTES

Rising Water is set the night of August 29 and the early morning of August 30, 2005, hours after Hurricane Katrina has passed the city. *Shotgun* opens in December 2005 in New Orleans, about four months after the collapse of Federal levees and the subsequent flooding. *Mold* is set the morning of Sunday, August 27, 2006.

Delacroix Island is pronounced "Dell-uh-craw." LaPlace is pronounced as in French ("Lah-Plahss"). Godchaux, however, is pronounced "God-shaw." Because of similar patterns of immigration, the English spoken in New Orleans resembles Brooklynese as much as it does a southern accent.

Edmond "Doc" Souchon's recording of "If Ever I Cease to Love," the Mardi Gras anthem, is preferred by many New Orleanians. There are many versions available of "If the Ocean Were Whiskey" (often titled "Rye Whiskey") and "Goodnight, Irene," as there are of "My Home's Across the Smoky Mountains" (often titled "My Home's Across the Blue Ridge Mountains"). The Seeger Family recording of "My Home's Across the Smoky Mountains" is a traditional version.

ABOUT THE AUTHOR

John Biguenet's books include *The Torturer's Apprentice: Stories* and *Oyster*, a novel, as well as such award-winning plays as *The Vulgar Soul, Rising Water, Shotgun, Mold, Broomstick*, and *Night Train*, which he developed on a Studio Attachment at the National Theatre in London. An O. Henry Award winner for his short fiction, he has twice been elected president of the American Literary Translators Association. Named its first guest columnist by *The New York Times*, Biguenet chronicled in both columns and videos his return to New Orleans after its catastrophic flooding and the efforts to rebuild the city. Having served as poet in residence at the University of Arkansas at Little Rock and at the University of Texas at Dallas, he is currently the Robert Hunter Distinguished University Professor at Loyola University in New Orleans.

CPSIA information can be obtained
at www.ICGtesting.com
Printed in the USA
LVHW031749030120
642460LV00003B/242/P